# LGBTQ+
# ATHLETES
## CLAIM THE FIELD

### STRIVING FOR EQUALITY

**KIRSTIN CRONN-MILLS**
WITH AN INTRODUCTION BY
ALEX JACKSON NELSON

TWENTY-FIRST CENTURY BOOKS / MINNEAPOLIS

*This book is dedicated to all athletes who are still fighting to be who they are without harassment or struggle, and to the allies who support them unconditionally.*

Acknowledgments: Many thanks go to the athletes who contributed to this book—Alex Jackson Nelson (so much extra gratitude to Alex for all the help), Elliott Kunerth, Eric Lueshen, Amelia Gapin, Child M and her mother—and to Domenica Di Piazza for the opportunity to pull it all together. Many thanks also to Madeline Kopiecki and Kayla Pawek for editorial and research help.

Note to Readers: To keep up with the ever-changing world of LGBTQ+ sports, check Outsports.com on a regular basis. The site is regularly updated with new LGBTQ+ milestones.

Twenty-First Century Books
A division of Lerner Publishing Group, Inc.
241 First Avenue North
Minneapolis, MN 55401 USA

For reading levels and more information, look up this title at www.lernerbooks.com.

Main body text set in Gamma ITC Std Book 11/15.
Typeface provided by International Typeface Corp.

**Library of Congress Cataloging-in-Publication Data**

Names: Cronn-Mills, Kirstin, 1968– author.
Title: LGBTQ+ athletes claim the field : Striving for equality / Kirstin Cronn-Mills, with an introduction by Alex Jackson Nelson, MSW, LGSW.
Description: Minneapolis: Twenty-First Century Books, [2016] | Includes bibliographical references and index.
Identifiers: LCCN 2015036754| ISBN 9781467780124 (lb : alk. paper) | ISBN 9781512411393 (eb pdf)
Subjects: LCSH: Gay athletes—Juvenile literature. | Transgender athletes—Juvenile literature.
Classification: LCC GV708.8 .C76 2016 | DDC 796.086/64—dc23

LC record available at http://lccn.loc.gov/2015036754

Manufactured in the United States of America
1-37627-18724-2/23/2016

# TABLE OF CONTENTS

# WHY THIS BOOK
# MATTERS

In his professional life, Alex Jackson Nelson works with LGBTQ+ youth and coordinates trainings with schools, medical providers, and other service agencies that work with LGBTQ+ youth.

For the record, I'm a trans guy. This means I was assigned female at birth, and my gender identity is male. For as long as I can remember, I have identified as male, but because I was born and labeled female, my sex assigned at birth and gender identity did not match. I grew up being seen as a girl and experienced much of my life labeled and interacted with that way. I played women's basketball and softball in high school and college in the 1990s. I left the college I played for shortly after I started identifying as trans and turned my back on sports entirely with the belief that sports was just another space in my life where I would never fit in and get to be myself. After all, sports teams are for either men or women, so where did I fit in as a trans person? I didn't see myself represented in sports, and I didn't know that trans athletes existed.

Since college I haven't really participated in organized sports, but I'd like to. I miss the feeling of togetherness that team sports can foster in such an intense way, and I miss the self-discipline that belonging to a sports team requires. I spent most of my time as a young person practicing and playing sports. My dad was a college athlete and an amazing teacher. We spent most of our time together in batting cages, outside throwing the ball around, or shooting hoops. I was a strong athlete back then, and I miss that part of my identity.

These days I wake up early before work and go to the gym. I lift weights and sometimes run on the treadmill. Boring, I know! On occasion I participate in running events for local charities, and I like extreme endurance challenges with obstacles and mud that require teamwork for successful completion. Growing up as an athlete—being an athlete—is a huge part of what made me who I am today. But I don't claim the identity of athlete as my own since it has felt unimaginable to be trans and an athlete. I gave up playing team sports because of gender segregation, feeling as if I don't belong or fit on either team. Even now, after identifying as a trans man for almost twenty years, I don't feel comfortable playing on men's teams. Maybe it's because I was raised as a girl and have spent half of my life being perceived as one. The gender binary (either masculine or feminine) and norms (societal rules) of what men and women can or should do create a false difference between us.

I have played a few pickup games of basketball with a bunch of guys at my gym. While playing, I have not felt the sense of camaraderie I remember feeling when playing women's sports in high school and college. I assume this is because I am used to the cultural norm, communication style, and team building that takes place on women's teams. I have not signed up for local recreational sports leagues because they are often gender segregated and my only option now is to play on a men's team, which I'm thrilled about, and yet it still feels uncomfortable.

## "WHAT SPORTS DID YOU PLAY IN HIGH SCHOOL?"

That question seems quite simple to answer and can be a great conversation starter in many situations: while watching a friend's sporting event, chatting with coworkers, or gathering with strangers around the TV at a local restaurant. Sports and sporting events inevitably bring people together, creating a unique camaraderie for athletes and those who enjoy supporting them. For me, as a trans person, the question, "What sports did you play in high school?" often brings feelings of fear, anxiety, sadness, and anything *but* an opening for an easy connection.

I often reminisce about and appreciate all the lessons I learned from participating in sports during high school and college. My experience as an athlete enabled me to learn important things about myself and how to support others. If I wasn't a trans person, questions about my participation in sports would be an opportunity for me to connect with those who ask and maybe to brag about my past talents and abilities as an athlete. When this question comes up, however, I am forced to ask myself several complicated questions:

- DO I KNOW THE PERSON ASKING THE QUESTION WELL ENOUGH TO KNOW THAT THEY WILL ACCEPT ME AS A TRANS PERSON?

- AM I JUST STARTING A NEW JOB? WILL I GET FIRED FROM MY JOB FOR BEING HONEST ABOUT WHO I AM?

- IS THERE ANY POTENTIAL PHYSICAL RISK TO ME BY ANSWERING HONESTLY (TELLING THEM THAT I PLAYED SOFTBALL AND COMING OUT AS TRANS)?

- IF I DECIDE TO DODGE THE QUESTION, HOW MUCH OF MYSELF AM I WILLING TO OVERLOOK TO FALSELY CONNECT WITH THE PERSON ASKING THE QUESTION?

- AM I IN A LOCKER ROOM AT THE GYM? IS IT SAFE TO BE HONEST HERE?

Beyond opportunities for social connection and recognition, sports can bring us self-confidence and a sense of achievement. Sports teach us that hard work and practice, over a period of time, lead to success in reaching our goals. We are able to see ourselves excel, get better at something, and feel proud of ourselves. Sometimes people get scholarships to college for playing sports and build careers as professional athletes making a living playing the game they love. Sports also contribute to our health and well-being, and as a young person, they teach us how to successfully build relationships, counting on one another for support and success.

Whether we are currently playing, talking about our past playing careers, or if we've never played and are talking about our favorite teams, playing and watching sports has a way of bringing people together. Sports teams are sometimes made up of strangers coming together to create shared goals, failing and succeeding together, because of one another. Every member is needed on a team to be successful. Every person counts. As a trans person who has often felt as if I didn't belong, especially in middle and high school, sports gave me the sense of belonging that I needed to survive.

Many lesbian, gay, bisexual, transgender, queer/questioning, and other (LGBTQ+) athletes are like me. They grow up feeling that they don't belong. They have to weigh risk factors when answering questions about themselves and their history. They may not feel safe talking openly about their gender identity or their sexual orientation. They may fear ridicule, physical and emotional injury, or they may fear getting kicked off a team—or not accepted onto the team in the first place.

## MOVING TOWARD EQUITY

So why does inequity and hostility toward LGBTQ+ athletes in sports organizations exist in the first place? I believe it is rooted in prejudice and discrimination toward and against LGBTQ+ people. Prejudice can keep us from getting to know and support one another. Prejudicial thoughts come from negative stereotypes, things we have heard or learned from others that are most often not true about a group of people who are different from us (whoever that "us" might be). They are maintained by society and often lead to fear and hatred toward others. That fear can cause us to do discriminatory things to other people, such as calling them hurtful names or not allowing them to play on a sports team because they are different from us.

Throughout history, LGBTQ+ people around the world have felt the need to hide their true selves and identities because of prejudice and discrimination. Prejudice and discrimination have profoundly impacted how we (LGBTQ+ people) live our lives and how we feel about ourselves, whether at home alone, when going to work, or while playing a game of football with friends down the street. Some LGBTQ+ people feel the need to hide loving relationships from family and close friends because we are afraid that our family will not approve or will disown us. We might feel we need to hide our identities from others because we can lose our jobs and housing as LGBTQ+ people. In twenty-nine states in the United States, people can be fired from their jobs or kicked out of their apartments for being gay, lesbian, or bisexual. This is true in thirty-two states for transgender people.

The good news is that we can all play a role in ending prejudice and discrimination by getting to know LGBTQ+ people and transforming societal thinking that creates prejudices. A shift in societal beliefs in the United States has allowed LGBTQ+ people more legal rights than in the past. With the June 2015 Supreme Court ruling in *Obergefell v. Hodges*, the US Supreme Court ruled in favor of same-sex marriage across the nation. In some states, trans folks can legally change their birth names and gender markers to reflect their true gender identity on state identification forms and are protected through civil rights antidiscrimination legislation. Health care by LGBTQ+-friendly and competent providers is more accessible than in the past. Negative stereotypes and social beliefs about LGBTQ+ people are changing thanks to the tireless work of people willing to challenge social constructs of prejudice. The history of LGBTQ+ movements and the trailblazers leading fights for equity and justice are important to acknowledge and celebrate while continuing to fight for justice and equity.

When I was an athlete in high school and college, being transgender *and* an athlete on a team was impossible. There was no place for me in sports. Today state high school leagues and colleges have established policies for transgender athletes. I am claiming my field by reclaiming my history as a trans athlete, even if I wasn't able to be my authentic trans self when playing sports back then. I'm asking readers to treat me and other LGBTQ+ athletes with dignity, fairness, and equity. To celebrate us as athletes who bring skill, compassion, commitment, and moxie to the game and to sports organizations.

My hope is that we all, as human beings, have the ability to be and bring our true and authentic selves to the sports we enjoy. Equity means we don't have to hide pieces of ourselves for fear that we will lose friends, family, kids, our team, our jobs, or the interest of a stranger who asks us, "What sports did you play in high school?" Claiming equity for LGBTQ+ athletes will include claiming our fields in every sport possible.

—ALEX JACKSON NELSON

About his decision to come out publicly as a gay man, first baseman David Denson said, "Talking with my teammates, they gave me the confidence I needed, coming out to them."

# CHAPTER ONE

# POWER, PRIDE–
# AND PREJUDICE

In August 2015, minor-league baseball player David Denson came out. Not as a strong first baseman, not as a high-average hitter (batting .253 at that point in his season), but as a gay man. He was the first player affiliated with Major League Baseball (MLB) to come out while actively playing. And he did it with the support of his organization, the Milwaukee Brewers. He also had the support of former player Billy Bean, a gay man who came out in 1999, after retirement, and who was appointed MLB's Ambassador for Inclusion in 2014. According to a formal statement from Major League Baseball, "[The Brewers' support for Denson] is a tremendous example of baseball's desire to give every player the opportunity to play at their very best."

Like Denson and Bean, lesbian, gay, bisexual, transgender, queer/questioning, and other (LGBTQ+) athletes seem to be everywhere: coming out, getting engaged, getting married, and kissing their spouses on national TV. In 2015, for example, women's basketball star Brittney Griner got married to—and split from—her fellow Women's National Basketball Association (WNBA) player and girlfriend Glory Johnson. British Olympic diver Tom Daley announced his engagement to screenwriter Dustin Lance Black in the *London Times*. Michigan high school athlete Matt Dils came out as gay, inspired by the example set by other out athletes.

Just three months before Denson's announcement, the world's first multinational survey about homophobia in sports was released. Commissioned by the Bingham Cup Sydney 2014, a gay rugby World Cup, and conducted by global sports market research firm Repucom, the report is known as *Out on the Fields*. The survey polled almost ninety-five hundred participants in six English-speaking countries (the United States, United Kingdom, Australia, Canada, Ireland, and New Zealand). The participants identify as straight or as lesbian, gay, or bisexual (LGB). (No transgender or intersex people were involved in the study.) According to the survey participants, gay men in these nations feel least comfortable in the United States. The report notes, "When broken down by country, the USA and Australia stood out as the countries in which gay men felt the least welcome in sport, with nearly 60% believing they are 'not accepted at all' or 'accepted a little.'" Additionally, it's still a huge deal to be a gay, lesbian, or bisexual athlete, especially for young people. As the survey report states, "The overwhelming majority of participants (73%), including straight participants, did not believe that youth sport was welcoming and safe [for LGB participants]."

So what's going on? Are LGBTQ+ athletes welcomed in their sports, or do they feel unsafe and unaccepted as out athletes? Turns out both things are true.

## A WATERSHED MOMENT

Sports are part of the cultural fabric of the United States, and athletes are among the people Americans admire the most. We value athletes for their physical prowess, the contributions they make to their sports, and the reinforcement they provide to the American sense of national pride. Athletes have been considered heroes

Brittney Griner, a center for the Phoenix Mercury, was the first NCAA basketball player ever to score two thousand points and block five hundred shots. She came out as a lesbian in 2013, saying that her parents gave her the courage to be open about her sexuality.

for a long time, almost as long as human beings have been competing in sports events. In ancient Greece, for example, athletes modeled themselves after their mythic heroes. They watched players compete in the ancient Olympic Games, which date back to 776 BCE.

Are Americans of the twenty-first century ready to call LGBTQ+ athletes heroes? Many people, athletes and fans alike, saw Michael Sam as just that. Sam changed the landscape of professional sports—especially football, one of the most masculine sports around—by coming out at a time when everyone expected him to remain silent.

Michael Sam spent his college football career as a defensive end, taking offensive players to the ground. Sam played for the University of Missouri (Mizzou) Tigers for four years and won national awards in his senior year. Draft experts assumed he would go on to play professional ball and that he would be chosen by a National Football League (NFL) team early in the 2014 draft. But Sam had an open secret: he is gay. His team and coaches knew, and word began to filter out as it got closer to the NFL draft. To remain in control of the story, Sam told the sports world his news in February 2014. Sam made history. No Division I football player had ever come out while still active in his sport. NFL player Dave Kopay, who played from 1964 to 1972, was the first football player to claim his gay identity, but he did so in 1975, three years after he had retired. Michael Sam wasn't going to wait until after retirement.

Sam was the 249th player of 256 to be drafted in the 2014 NFL Draft, and he went to the St. Louis Rams. His "draft moment" was a lot like every other player's moment. He looked surprised and proud, and then he kissed his loved one—his longtime partner Vito Cammisano. All of a sudden, the NFL was different, and so was the sporting world. Michael Sam had claimed his identity as a gay man and as a football player. President Barack Obama congratulated Sam for his bravery, and Sam was awarded the Arthur Ashe Courage Award in summer 2014. ABC (American Broadcasting Company) and ESPN (Entertainment and Sports Programming Network) give this award each year as part of the ESPY (Excellence in Sports Performance Yearly), to honor athletes whose humanitarian contribution transcends the sports world.

However, Michael Sam's professional football career was marked by struggle. The St. Louis Rams released him at the end of August 2014 when the team made its final cuts to the roster. Although the Dallas Cowboys picked up Sam for their practice squad, he was soon released, in October 2014. The next spring, he participated in the first NFL Veteran Combine (a place for unsigned NFL veterans to try out for teams) but wasn't signed to a team. In summer 2015, Sam signed with the Montreal Alouettes, of the Canadian Football League. He left the team in August 2015 citing mental health reasons.

Why did Sam struggle? Many observers believe it was the stress of being the first openly gay man in the NFL. LGBTQ+ players face tremendous pressures, prejudice, and discrimination. According to the executive summary of the *Campus Pride 2012 LGBTQ National College Athlete Report*, this discrimination takes several forms, including

verbal harassment, derogatory remarks on electronic media, and being pressured to be silent about identity issues. Harassment can happen at practice, during competitions, and in on-campus housing. Coaches and other student-athletes are usually the perpetrators of harassment. At the professional level, discrimination can include disqualification from participation because of perceived inappropriate sexual behavior or the inability to garner lucrative endorsements.

In 2015, about a year after NFL defensive end Michael Sam *(left)* came out as a gay man, he competed on *Dancing with the Stars*. Sam acknowledged the support of his then fiancé, swimmer Vito Cammisano *(right)*, in being public about his sexuality.

At all levels of participation, fans may be critical, dismissive, or hateful toward a competitor because of gender identity or sexual orientation.

## HOMOPHOBIA, TRANSPHOBIA, AND MISOGYNY

Why does society make it hard for LGBTQ+ athletes to claim their authentic selves? The driving forces behind discrimination against LGBTQ+ athletes are homophobia and transphobia. Homophobia is a strong hatred or fear of individuals who are lesbian, gay, or bisexual, or of individuals in a same-sex couple. Transphobia involves a strong hatred or fear of individuals who are transgender. Homophobia and transphobia are usually linked to a belief that same-sex attraction and aligning a person's bodily presentation with that person's brain gender are unnatural or immoral. Misogyny also plays a part in discrimination. Misogyny is an expressed dislike for or contempt for women, based on a cultural attitude that sees women as weaker and less capable than men.

## INTERSECTIONALITY AND COMING OUT

Every human on the planet has more than one identity. LGBTQ+ athletes are also fathers, mothers, sisters, brothers, children, and parents. Intersectionality theory is the study of how identities—racial, sexual, gender, and others—come together, especially in relation to oppression, discrimination, and prejudice.

Sometimes an athlete may have several marginalized identities that lead to discrimination. If she is a lesbian of color, for instance, both of these identities may play a role in her decision about whether to come out—or not to come out. She may feel it would be hard—and possibly damaging to her career—to come out, because of the possibility of racism as well as homophobia. If an LGBTQ+ athlete has a disability, that person will have to consider the possibility of discrimination against the disability combined with homophobia.

Demographics and economics can make a difference too. For example, an athlete in a small town might not choose to come out, while an athlete in a major urban area might do so. Smaller towns often have fewer LGBTQ+ residents and less support to offer a LGBTQ+ player. LGBTQ+ athletes must always assess the risks and benefits of coming out. It is still a courageous choice to do so.

Homophobia, transphobia, and misogyny are expressed through social policies (for example, medical care for transgender individuals that is not covered by insurance plans or for which practitioners are unprepared or lack knowledge) and religious practices (such as churches that exclude homosexual or transgender members). They are also expressed as physical, verbal, or emotional violence against women or against individuals who are LGBTQ+. Add stereotypes—easy and often wildly inaccurate categorizations of individuals—to homophobia, transphobia, and misogyny, and you have a very powerful recipe for unfair treatment of LGBTQ+ people, including athletes.

## SCIENCE AND SOCIALIZATION

Some Americans believe that same-sex attraction is morally or physically wrong. Yet science is increasingly telling us that same-sex attraction may be a biological variance in our genes, just like being left-handed or having blue eyes. A study published in 2014 in the *Quarterly Review of Biology* finds that some genes' sensitivity to the hormone testosterone is temporarily altered by biochemical factors called epi-marks. These epi-marks may regulate the amount of testosterone to which a fetus is exposed. Medical researchers point to testosterone exposure in the womb as one of the possible biological influences on same-sex attraction.

Similarly, researchers are finding a scientific basis for being transgender, which is often though not always defined as a mismatch between a human's brain-determined gender identity and the sex, based on anatomical features, to which a doctor assigns that person at birth. Many brain and body variations exist under the transgender label, and researchers are discovering new biological foundations for these variations all the time.

Biology is only part of the picture. As individuals grow up, they learn about social norms from the people around them—their families, neighbors, classmates, and friends, as well as the media.

They learn what it means to be male and female and how to express that identity. They learn whom to bond with romantically and which relationships are valued over others. Sports can be part of that powerful socialization process, especially for boys. Dr. Pat Griffin is a former teacher, coach, and athlete, and is one of the world's leading LGBTQ+ activists and researchers. She is a recognized expert in the United States and Canada about the issues pertaining to LGBTQ+ athlete inclusion. Her research and writing focus on heterosexism and homophobia in education and athletics. (Heterosexism is the belief that opposite-sex attractions and relationships are superior to any other kind of relationships.) According to Griffin, sports are part of the way culture defines and develops the notion of masculinity. She says,

> Sport is more than games. As an institution, sport serves important social functions in supporting conventional social values. In particular, sport is a training ground where boys learn what it means to be men. Masculinity does not come naturally; it must be carefully taught. Specific rewards and punishments provide clear messages about acceptable and unacceptable behavior for boys. Boys who show an interest in "girl" activities, such as playing with dolls, dancing, or cooking, are teased by peers. Young boys learn at an early age that participation in athletics is an important, if not required, part of developing a masculine identity and gaining acceptance among peers.

Yet if male athletes are suspected or known to be gay, they face cultural stereotypes that say that gay men are not masculine or that they are too weak and feminine to compete. According to Griffin, "A gay male athlete violates both the image of male athletes as strong, virile, and heterosexual and the image of gay men as swishy and effeminate. . . . If gay men can be strong, tough, competitive, and part of a male bonding experience in the locker room with straight men, how can straight men confidently differentiate themselves from gay men?"

Sports exert very different socialization pressures on girls and women, however. Social values expect women to be feminine, attractive, delicate, and not too strong. For women and girls, the challenge is to find a way into sports and to cultivate power and strength despite social influences that tend to restrict these qualities to male athletes. In fact, women who participate in sports are often viewed automatically as lesbians, in part because powerful female participation in sports challenges strongly held notions of gender expression and gender performance. According to Griffin,

> *Women's serious participation in sport brings into question the "natural" and mutually exclusive nature of gender and gender roles. If women in sport can be tough minded, competitive, and muscular too, then sport loses its special place in the development of masculinity for men. If women can so easily develop these so-called masculine qualities, then what are the meanings of femininity and masculinity? What does it mean to be a man or a woman?*

## RECRUITING AND TEAM DYNAMICS

Cultural prejudices about sexual and gender identity play out at the deepest levels of sporting organizations. In professional sports, for example, coaches and organizational staff work hard to build a winning team. They look for players with good performance records and the potential to bring money and pride to the franchise. They often pay huge amounts of money to woo players, signing them for lucrative, multimillion-dollar deals. Careers and money hang in the balance, so teammates, families, and the media carefully scrutinize recruiting. Because the stakes are so high, recruiting can be especially difficult for LGBTQ+ players. Athletes often feel they must hide their true identities so as not to upset or scare away recruiters, as well as future teammates and their families. For example, star WNBA player Brittney Griner, a lesbian and one of the most gifted women basketball players of all time, revealed that while she was playing for Baylor University—a small Christian college in Texas—head coach Kim Mulkey did not allow the members of the women's basketball team to publicly discuss their sexuality. "It was a recruiting thing," Griner told ESPN. "The coaches thought that if it seemed like they condoned [homosexuality], people wouldn't let their kids come play for Baylor." This practice of creating a "stay away" message related to lesbian players or coaches is part of a strategy known as negative recruiting. Coaches point to other teams with lesbian players while focusing on the so-called family values of their own team as a way to signal their rejection of homosexuality and to promote their team as a place of safety. Yet negative recruiting typically doesn't happen in men's sports, because everyone generally (and wrongly) assumes that all players are straight.

Some coaches have been very public about negative recruiting. For example, the very successful women's basketball coach Maureen (Rene) Portland, formerly at Pennsylvania State University, claimed she wouldn't have any homosexuality in her program. Her discriminatory practice was unquestioned until 2007. That year Portland chose to resign after settling

Many sports teams have had unofficial but rigidly enforced anti-LGBTQ+ policies. For example, players have said that head women's basketball coach Kim Mulkey (right) of Baylor University does not allow lesbian players to openly discuss their sexuality.

a lawsuit with a former Penn State player against whom Portland had discriminated because Portland had assumed the player was a lesbian.

Coaches too can be the victims of harmful stereotyping and discrimination. For example, in September 2015, three openly lesbian head coaches at the University of Minnesota Duluth filed a lawsuit alleging they were fired from their coaching jobs because of their gender and sexual orientation. Shannon Miller (hockey), Jen Banford (softball), and Annette Wiles (basketball) claim they were harassed, suffered from a hostile work environment, and were denied pay comparable to the coaches of men's teams at the university. According to Miller, "Sexism and homophobia are alive and well at the University of Minnesota." Former University of Minnesota associate women's golf coach Katie Brenny can vouch for that. After she was hired in 2010, she was demoted and assigned to tasks below her qualifications. She was also told to stay away from students. What changed? The people she worked for discovered she was a lesbian. Brenny sued the university, claiming that the university had violated Minnesota's Human Rights Act, which outlaws discrimination based on sexual orientation. Brenny won a monetary settlement in March 2014.

Pat Griffin wrote about this kind of discrimination in a piece for *Outsports*, an online publication about LGBTQ+ athletes and athletics. The article covered a group of coaches who sued their colleges for discrimination. As Griffin says, "If you are

Former women's hockey coach Shannon Miller *(left)* of the University of Minnesota Duluth—along with former softball coach Jen Banford and former women's basketball coach Annette Wiles—filed a lawsuit seeking $18 million in damages for discrimination based on age, gender, sexual orientation, and national origin. The suit is likely to go to trial in 2017.

a lesbian coach, the message is, you better watch your back, keep it on the down low and even if you do stay in the closet, when athletic administrators want to come for your job, they will find a reason to justify their action."

Team dynamics are also affected by homophobia. In fall 2012, Minnesota Vikings special teams coordinator Mike Priefer commented before a special teams meeting: "We should round up all the gays, send them to an island, and then nuke it until it glows." He made the statement in the presence of Vikings punter Chris Kluwe, a straight man and an LGBTQ+ ally, who objected to the remark. Kluwe had gone on record in summer 2012 in support of defeating a referendum that would have made same-sex marriage illegal in Minnesota. He had received clearance from the Vikings team to go public with his views, as a private citizen, but had then been asked to tone down his ally activism and pay attention to his punting. The Vikings released Kluwe from his contract in May 2013. Kluwe feels it was because of his very public LGBTQ+ activism. The Vikings disagreed, saying his release was strictly due to poor performance. Kluwe, who threatened to sue the Vikings over his release, settled with the team after the Vikings agreed to donate money to LGBTQ+ charities. After an investigation into Priefer's homophobic remarks, the team suspended him for three games in 2014.

## FAN PERCEPTIONS AND PRODUCT ENDORSEMENTS

Homophobia and transphobia are realities of the sporting world. Yet there are some safe spaces for LGBTQ+ athletes, in part because of their fans. For example, one of the WNBA's largest and most enduring fan bases is LGBTQ+. No other franchised sport can make such a claim. In June 2014, the WNBA became the first sports league to actively market toward this fan base. The campaign included a WNBA Pride logo, merchandise, player appearances at Pride events, and a Pride game between the Tulsa Shock and the Chicago Sky.

## WHAT ABOUT LOCKER ROOMS?

Sports are one of the most segregated segments of culture. For the most part, especially in the professional world, teams and competitions are organized by gender: men play for one team or organization, and women play for another. Locker room assignments are based on both gender and sex. One locker room belongs to women and another to men. To have access to a locker room, teams expect players in each locker room to have the same anatomy. In locker rooms, players dress and undress, shower, talk, discuss team performance, and celebrate victories.

After Michael Sam came out as a gay man, locker rooms were part of the national discussion surrounding his revelation. Some Americans were worried. They asked if locker rooms could be a place of violence against gay men or for gay men to approach and convert straight men. In an article for ESPN called "Nothing to See Here: A History of Showers in Sports," journalist David Fleming investigated the issue. He concluded that NFL locker rooms, like other locker rooms, are for celebrations, team meetings, and showering, but not a place for sexual behavior or for violence against gay men. According to Fleming, "Getting clean next to a gay teammate is probably one of the more ordinary things that happen in the team shower. And if there's one universal certainty in a sports shower, it's this: Everyone's looking."

While there may be looking going on, that's as far as it goes. Jo-Lonn Dunbar, Sam's former teammate with the St. Louis Rams, had this to say, "Look, guys shower together. . . . And Sam's been showering with

Quarterback Eli Manning (center) talks to his New York Giants teammates in the team's locker room after their one-hundredth win in October 2015. Locker rooms are often a flashpoint in the discussion of LGBTQ+ participation in sports, even though players say that locker rooms are simply for preparing for games, celebrating, and talking.

guys forever. We haven't had any issues. . . . I don't know what people think or what their perception is of a team shower, but it's really not that cool. You just kind of get in there and get clean and just drop drawers. If everybody hasn't moved on from this already, they should now."

## BASELESS ASSUMPTIONS

When people worry about the locker room issue, they are supporting these two false stereotypes:

1. Athletes attracted to individuals of the same sex will not be able to control their actions in a locker room full of naked people. These athletes will see the locker room as an opportunity to seduce other teammates.
2. Our genitals determine our gender. Locker rooms that allow people with the same gender but different genitals will lead to sexual violence. Transgender women with penises will be tempted to rape women with vaginas in the women's locker room. Or men with penises will be tempted to rape a transgender man with a vagina.

More than anything, these stereotypes reflect a cultural obsession with sex and the assumption that sexuality is a part of human behavior that individuals cannot control. Sometimes players call out the distressing insult behind these falsehoods. For example, retired basketball superstar Charles Barkley says that he played alongside gay players, with no problems in the locker rooms. He commented that "it's an insult to gay people to think that they are going to be looking at their teammates in a sexual way. That's an insult to all gay men."

LGBTQ+ fans had been fighting for recognition for some time. In August 2002, for example, a group known as Lesbians for Liberty organized a protest during a New York Liberty WNBA game. The goal of the protest was to ask the New York Liberty team to publicly acknowledge their lesbian fan base. During the game, lesbian fans kissed and displayed banners critical of the organization's silence toward lesbian fans. One protester wore a trench coat and a hat and covered her face with gauze. Her sandwich-board sign read The Invisible Fan. The sign also featured a pink triangle, a symbol of lesbian and gay oppression echoing back to the Nazi death camps of World War II (1939–1945), where gay and lesbian prisoners were forced to wear pink triangles on their shirts.

Not all lesbian WNBA fans supported the protest. Some felt it took away from the real point of the event: playing basketball. Why did the sexual orientation of the fans matter? they wondered. To respond to the debate, the Liberty team issued a statement saying that Liberty games were a place where all fans were treated equally.

For a while, the WNBA had a celebrity couple in Brittney Griner and Glory Johnson, who announced their engagement in August 2014, married in May 2015, and split in June 2015. Griner and Johnson were even featured in a 2015 episode of the TV show *Say Yes to the Dress: Atlanta*, as Johnson searched for a wedding dress for the upcoming wedding ceremony.

The WNBA isn't the only sport whose fans welcome out players. Women's soccer had at least seventeen out players and coaches in the 2015 World Cup games. Two of those players, Megan Rapinoe and Abby Wambach, were featured prominently in the US women's team advertising campaign during the World Cup. The coach of the US team, Jill Ellis, is also openly gay. According to soccer fan Ashley Evans, soccer fans don't take these role models and heroes for granted. She says, "I think it's really powerful [to have out players and coaches] and sends a great message to people who might not be accepting of LGBT inclusion and also to young soccer players . . . if they see these women speaking out for them, saying, hey we need to be inclusive of everybody no matter who they love or what their orientation is, just having role models is so powerful and important."

When the US Supreme Court ruled in favor of same-sex marriage in all fifty states in June 2015, the United States Soccer Federation sent this tweet, complete with a header picture of an eagle and the rainbow-colored words ONE NATION ONE TEAM: "More than ever today, we are #OneNationOneTeam. #LoveWins."

While the US soccer world is very inclusive of lesbians, no players on the US men's national soccer team are out (though there may not be any gay players on the team at this time). In Major League Soccer (MLS), only one player is out—Robbie Rogers. He joined the LA Galaxy, an MLS team, in May 2013. In June 2013, Rogers came out through a post on his personal website. Then he joined basketball player Jason Collins as one of the first two out athletes in all five major North American sports leagues (Major League Baseball, the National Basketball Association, the National Football League, the National Hockey League, and Major League Soccer). Megan Rapinoe has noted the difference between coming out as a gay man and coming out as a lesbian woman. She said, "I feel like sports in general are still homophobic, in the sense that not a lot of people are out. . . . In female sports, if you're gay, most likely your team knows it pretty quickly. It's very open and widely supported. For males, it's not that way at all. It's sad."

The landscape for LGBTQ+ athletes is evolving fast, and athletes continue to come out. However, LGBTQ+ athletes still face hurdles to equal access to athletic competition and fair play. Nonetheless, the LGBTQ+ sports world is exciting—and it's constantly growing and changing, with many gains already achieved and many still to come.

Jill Ellis, at a soccer match in Florida, is the head coach of the US women's national soccer team. She is openly lesbian and married her girlfriend Betsy Stephenson in 2013.

Cameras around the world caught the moment when US women's soccer star Abby Wambach *(standing)* kissed her wife, Sarah Huffman, after the US women's team won the FIFA Women's World Cup championship in 2015.

# CHAPTER TWO

# ATHLETES COME OUT

In summer 2015, US national women's soccer player Abby Wambach made history. In June and July of that year, the US women's soccer team competed for the FIFA Women's World Cup in Canada. On July 5, they claimed a decisive victory in Vancouver, British Columbia, beating Japan 5–2 in the final game of the tournament. As the players celebrated on the field, forward Abby Wambach raced to the sidelines to kiss and embrace her wife, soccer player Sarah Huffman. This celebratory moment came just a week after the US Supreme Court had declared same-sex marriage to be legal in all fifty states. The kiss was the ultimate affirmation for many fans of progress toward LGBTQ+ rights. As fan and BuzzFeed reporter Ellie Hall put it on Twitter, "ABBY WAMBACH KISSING HER WIFE, A UNION NOW RECOGNIZED THROUGHOUT THE USA, IS A PRETTY NICE ENDING TO THIS WORLD CUP."

Wambach's teammate Megan Rapinoe came out in 2012, after her team (the US national women's soccer team) became the runner-up in the 2011 FIFA Women's World Cup and before the team's gold medal performance in the 2012 Olympic Games in London, England. She became engaged to her girlfriend, singer-songwriter Sera Cahoone, about a month after the team's decisive victory in the 2015 FIFA Women's World Cup. Rapinoe shared the news of her engagement— and a photo of the couple—on Instagram to more than 430,000 followers. Neither Rapinoe nor Wambach seems to get negative attention from fellow players, team officials, fans, or the media.

Yet for Michael Sam, coming out was not smooth sailing. After he went public with his sexual orientation, he was drafted; cut from two NFL teams (the St. Louis Rams and the Dallas Cowboys); and left a third football team, the Montreal Alouettes. Did his choice to be open about his identity hurt his career possibilities? The owner of the Dallas Cowboys, Jerry Jones, said that Sam's sexuality was a non-issue to the team. Was that true for others in the NFL? One thing is clear: Michael Sam's decision to claim his identity still ripples through the NFL and gives pause to other LGBTQ+ players in the league, who may now be reconsidering whether to make that same decision for themselves.

## EARLY ATHLETES WHO CLAIMED THEIR FIELDS

LGBTQ+ athletes have played and competed as long as there have been athletes. However, LGBTQ+ athletes have not always been out and proud. It has only been since about 2010 that large numbers of American athletes have begun to claim their LGBTQ+ identities publicly. Up until then, not many have felt safe enough to face the scrutiny, pressures, hateful language, and discrimination from other players, fans, organizations, and the media.

According to historians, the first out athlete in the United States was likely tennis great Bill Tilden (William Tatem Tilden II). He never hid his sexuality from others during his professional playing years, in which he won three singles titles at Wimbledon, in 1920, 1921, and 1930. Tilden also won seven US championships, plus a few team titles. Tilden was ranked number one in the world in the 1920s. After he retired from tennis, he published an autobiography—*My Story: A Champion's Memoirs*—in 1948, in which he came out publicly as gay. In reaction to the news, the Germantown, Pennsylvania, Cricket Club, of which he had been a longtime member, canceled his membership. The University of Pennsylvania, in his hometown of Philadelphia and from which he had graduated, removed his name from the list of alumni. After his public admission of his homosexuality, he never regained

his prominence. He died of heart complications in 1953.

About twenty years later, in 1975, Dave Kopay became the first American professional player to publicly acknowledge a romantic relationship with another man. Kopay had been an All-American running back with the Washington Huskies football team at the University of Washington and was a cocaptain of the university's 1964 Rose Bowl team. He had played professional football with five NFL teams during his eight-year career and had been retired for three years when he revealed his homosexuality in an interview with the *Washington Star* newspaper. After Kopay came out, he says he did not experience any backlash. However, no players, coaches, or NFL staff publicly supported him. And the newspapers and television and radio shows that carried the story all received negative mail—more than with any other story they had ever run—about Kopay's decision to come out and about the media's decision to run with the story. Nobody was ready to hear about a gay athlete in 1975.

Why did Kopay come out? In Eric Marcus's book *Making History: The Struggle for Gay and Lesbian Equal Rights, 1945-1990, an Oral*

*History*, Marcus quotes Kopay, who said he had seen an article in the *Washington Star* in December 1975 about homosexual athletes who discussed all they had to lose by coming out. Kopay noticed that all the gay athletes in the article chose to be anonymous. While reading the article, he recognized one of the players in the article as Jerry Smith, a tight end for the Washington Redskins, who was still playing for the NFL at the time of the article's publication. In his football career with the Redskins, Smith had set a league record for most touchdown catches for a tight end (sixty), and he went to the

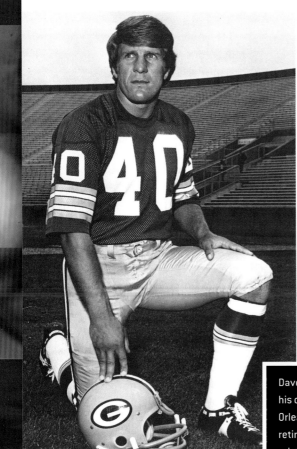

Pro Bowl twice. Kopay and Smith had had a brief relationship, and Kopay was saddened that Smith hadn't felt safe enough to come out. According to Kopay, "I was at a time and place in my own coming out where I felt that if I was going to survive, I had to speak out. It was do that or maybe go crazy." As a retired player, Kopay also felt he had less to lose than other athletes seeking endorsements: "I didn't have the . . . beer commercial to lose," he pointed out.

Kopay was feeling something much larger, and in coming out, he became a pioneer for other gay athletes. According to Kopay,

Dave Kopay played for five football teams during his career: San Francisco, Detroit, Washington, New Orleans, and Green Bay *(left)*. He came out in 1975 after retiring from the sport. Kopay has said that his brief relationship with tight end Jerry Smith was his first true coming-out experience.

*I felt that [coming out] was something I could do. I didn't feel like any big hero or any big courageous dude or any of that stuff. I felt, Dammit! I can do something here and I know it's important because I wish I had that kind of person to read about when I was younger.*

Kopay did pay a price for going public with his sexuality. For example, after retiring from professional sports, he had hoped to get a coaching job, as retired athletes often do. Yet no one approached him for such a position. So instead, he wrote a memoir, *The Dave Kopay Story* (1977). In his book, Kopay mentioned his sexual encounter with Smith, though he did not name him. Smith never spoke to Kopay again. Kopay tried to make a living with speaking engagements. Eventually he ended up with a job as a salesperson and buyer for his uncle's flooring store in Los Angeles, California.

Kopay says that after he came out, the NFL never acknowledged him or his book. In the early 1990s, he spoke about professional isolation:

*In all these years, I haven't heard a word from anybody in the NFL. Here I've been asked to speak in front of the American Bar Association [a professional organization for lawyers]. I was asked to go to San Francisco and be the keynote speaker at the [American Academy of Pediatrics] to talk to doctors and at least try to give them a glimpse of [a gay man] who they might be able to relate to. I've done a lot of creditable things toward improving the mental health of our society, yet the NFL still acts as if I don't exist, which pisses me off.*

In 2011 the online magazine *Outsports* did a feature series on the one hundred most important moments in gay sports history. The magazine ranked Dave Kopay's decision to come out as number one.

Kopay's choice to break the silence paved the way for many other athletes to do so.

## CLAIMING THE ULTIMATE PRIZE: FREEDOM

Tennis players Martina Navratilova and Billie Jean King were groundbreakers in women's tennis, not only as great players but because they too publicly claimed their sexual orientation at a time when it was risky to do so. Navratilova is the winner of fifty-nine Grand Slam titles, including nine Wimbledon singles titles. Billie Jean King holds thirty-nine Grand Slam titles, including six Wimbledon singles titles.

Navratilova came to the United States in 1975 from Czechoslovakia, her homeland and a Communist nation at the time. She defected

(left to go to a competitor or enemy nation) and applied for US citizenship. While her application was pending, she did not feel safe in revealing herself as a lesbian. Doing so could have disqualified her as a US citizen, she said. After her citizenship was granted in 1981, she gave an interview to journalist Steve Goldstein. She asked him to hold onto the information about her sexuality until she was ready to go public. However, Goldstein published a July 1981 story in the *New York Daily News* in which

Martina Navratilova on the court at Wimbledon in 1980. Navratilova is the author of her 1985 autobiography, titled *Martina*. In 2006 she published *Shape Your Self: My 6-Step Diet and Fitness Plan to Achieve the Best Shape of Your Life*. She married her partner Julia Lemigova in 2014.

he wrote about Navratilova's bisexuality. She later publicly identified herself as a lesbian.

Claiming her identity did not win Navratilova much respect. As a number one player in tennis at the time—and as an out lesbian—she did not get the wide range of lucrative endorsements that a player of her caliber would normally have received. Instead, she got endorsements for tennis rackets and other related gear rather than more lucrative deals to promote cars or clothes. Yet in 2013, Navratilova said that she had no regrets.

> I think because I came out and I was true to myself and was finally able to just be free and not have to pretend, not have to lie, not have to hide anything, I think because of that, I played better tennis, and, you know, of course, was a much happier person. So, I think it helped me become a better tennis player. Most of all, I felt free. And you can't put a price tag on that. Financially, did it cost me? Absolutely. How much? I don't know, and I really don't care.

On the other hand, American tennis legend Billie Jean King had no intention of coming out. According to King,

> I wanted to tell the truth [about my sexuality] but my parents were homophobic and I was in the closet. As well as that, I had people tell me that if I talked about what I was going through, it would be the end of the women's tour.
>
> I couldn't get a closet deep enough. I've got a homophobic family, a tour that will die if I come out, the world is homophobic and, yeah, I was homophobic. If you speak with gays, bisexuals, lesbians and [transgender individuals], you will find a lot of homophobia because of the way we all grew up.

Tennis champion Billie Jean King was in the closet for many years. She says, "I grew up homophobic. . . . I didn't get comfortable in my own skin until I was 51 about being gay." Since coming out, she has been a powerful, vocal advocate for gender equity and LGBTQ+ participation in sports.

By 1981, the year Navratilova came out, King had been married to Larry King, a lawyer and the founder of a major tennis organization, since 1965. She was doing her best to stay on top of her game. She was ranked number one in the world in women's tennis in 1966, 1967, 1968, 1971, 1972, and 1974. She had also won the Battle of the Sexes, a highly publicized tennis match and media event against male tennis player Bobby Riggs, in 1973. Yet King was living a double life, having started a romantic relationship with her secretary, Marilyn Barnett, in 1971. Barnett and King eventually split, and in 1981, Barnett sued King for monetary support, thereby outing one of the biggest stars of women's tennis. Billie Jean King lost all of her endorsements overnight.

After the lawsuit, King retired from singles play in 1983 and from doubles play in 1990. She remained married to her husband until 1987. King remained active in tennis for many years, coaching the Olympic women's team in 1996 and 2000. She officially came out, on her own terms, in 1998 and received belated accolades for her courage as an out lesbian athlete. For example, she received the Arthur Ashe Courage Award in 1999 and was inducted into the Chicago Gay and Lesbian Hall of Fame that same year. In 2000 she received an award from GLAAD (formerly the Gay & Lesbian Alliance Against Defamation), a media organization dedicated to promoting equality and acceptance for LGBTQ+ individuals, for her work as an advocate for the LGBTQ+ community. She has been partnered with Ilana Kloss, another women's tennis player and the commissioner of World Team Tennis, for more than thirty years. President Obama appointed King as part of the 2014 Olympic delegation to Sochi, Russia, but she withdrew because of her mother's failing health.

The year before, in 2013, King struck up a friendship with professional basketball player Jason Collins after he came out as a gay man. Collins is the first active player in any of the five major American sports leagues to come out. He simply and eloquently made history in a cover story for *Sports Illustrated* by saying, "I'm a 34-year-old NBA center. I'm black. And I'm gay. I didn't set out to be the first openly gay athlete playing in a major American team sport. But since I am, I'm happy to start the conversation." Collins's experience is much different from King's. Collins came out on the cover of a major sporting magazine, in complete control of his message and of the timing. King was outed against her will and was unable to control the situation.

To other gay athletes, basketball player Jason Collins says, "Never be afraid or ashamed or have any fear to be your true authentic self."

King congratulated Collins on Twitter, and the two started a texting friendship. Later, in a 2014 lunch interview with the *New York Times*, where they met in person for the first time, King and Collins discussed their coming-out stories with journalist Philip Galanes. King commented that although her own situation had been horrible, she knew it would make a difference to someone like Jason Collins. She said, "That was my hope: that it would help somebody else. . . . Larry [King's husband] and the [public relations] people, nobody wanted me to come out. My lawyers denied the story [about the lesbian relationship] before they even asked me about it. But I fought for 48 hours to have that press conference. I needed to tell the truth [about the relationship with Barnett]."

## CONTROVERSIAL TRUTHS AND TOUGH MOMENTS

Even after Navratilova and King were out publicly, LGBTQ+ athletes were still struggling. Progress was very slow. Diana Nyad, a long-distance swimmer, writer, and sports commentator, has never hidden the fact that she is a lesbian. However, when she was with ABC as a commentator in the 1980s, company executives asked her not to bring her female partner to company social events.

Meanwhile, Olympic decathlete Tom Waddell decided to break new ground. Having struggled with his sexuality for many years, he turned to sports to prove his masculinity to himself. He eventually competed with the US Olympic team in the 1968 Olympic Games in Mexico City. Moving to San Francisco in the 1970s, he came across a gay bowling league and decided to create something similar on a much grander scale. In 1980 he came up with the idea for a Gay Olympic Games as a way to fight homophobia, break stereotypes, and offer hope and legitimacy to the gay community. The first Gay Games took place in San Francisco in 1982 and have been hosted on three different continents since then. The Games provide a place for LGBTQ+

athletes to compete at all levels (amateurs to professionals compete in the same events) and to foster a space of inclusiveness.

In 1982, right before the first set of events, the US Olympic Committee (USOC) sued the Gay Olympic Games. The USOC did not want to allow the Gay Olympic Games to use the word "Olympic" in its name, even though other sporting organizations, including the Special Olympics, had used this word in their organizational titles without challenge. The case went all the way to the US Supreme Court, which ruled in favor of the USOC in 1987. The event has been known as the Gay Games since that time.

## HIV/AIDS

In the early 1980s, doctors in New York and California began to observe unexplained illnesses in homosexual men and in people who injected drugs intravenously. Soon medical research teams identified the cause of the illnesses. The virus became known as human immunodeficiency virus (HIV), and HIV-related illnesses were called acquired immunodeficiency syndrome (AIDS). With no cures or treatment drugs at the time, a diagnosis of HIV or AIDS was a death sentence. Americans and much of the rest of the world were terrified of the disease, and drug users and homosexuals were stigmatized and faced discrimination in the workplace, in schools, and in society at large.

The world of competitive sports was not untouched by HIV/AIDS. Jerry Smith, who had been one of Dave Kopay's romantic partners, died of AIDS at the age of forty-three, in 1986. Smith remained in the closet until the end of his life, never acknowledging any relationships with men. In an article about Smith's fight with the illness, published in the *Washington Post* in 1986, journalist George Solomon wrote that "although Smith was willing to discuss his struggle with the disease, he would not elaborate on his life style."

Tom Waddell, founder of the Gay Games, was always open about his identity as a gay man. In 1986 he became one of the first US athletes to go public about his AIDS status. Waddell competed in Gay Games II in 1986, winning a gold medal in the men's javelin. He died in 1987, at the age of forty-nine.

In Major League Baseball, outfielder Glenn Burke is considered the first gay pioneer. He played for the Los Angeles Dodgers and the Oakland Athletics in the 1970s and never shied away from identifying as gay with his teammates and team owners. However, he left the game in 1980 because of prejudice and did not share his orientation with the public until the early 1980s, when his career was over and an article in *Inside Sports* magazine revealed his homosexuality. According to Burke, "Prejudice drove me out of baseball sooner than I should have [retired] . . . but I wasn't changing [my orientation]." Sportswriters suggest that because of homophobia, the Los Angeles Dodgers chose to trade him to the Oakland A's in 1978. Burke started regularly for the A's that year but didn't play in 1979 because of a pinched nerve in his neck. When he returned in 1980, team manager Billy Martin used derogatory language to introduce Burke to his teammates as a "faggot." Some teammates refused to shower with him. After his retirement, Burke went into a downward spiral, experiencing addiction, a devastating car accident, and isolation. He died of AIDS-related complications in 1995. In 2013 he was among the first group

Glenn Burke awaits the pitch at batting practice in Los Angeles in 1977 when he was with the Los Angeles Dodgers. When the team management learned of his homosexuality, which he did not hide, they offered him $75,000 to get married to a woman. He refused and was eventually traded to the Oakland A's, in 1978.

Greg Louganis prepares for a dive in 1983. Thirty years later, the four-time Olympic gold medalist married his partner, paralegal Johnny Chaillot, in a ceremony in Malibu, California.

of athletes to be inducted into the newly formed National Gay and Lesbian Sports Hall of Fame.

The year that Burke died, Olympic diver Greg Louganis went public with his homosexuality—and with his HIV-positive status—in an interview with Oprah Winfrey. Louganis faced criticism for not having gone public much earlier about being HIV positive, which he had known since the late 1980s. The criticism died down, and Louganis went on to write a best-selling autobiography, *Breaking the Surface*, in 1996, and to advocate for LGBTQ+ civil rights. Like Glenn Burke, Louganis was among the first group of US athletes to be inducted into the National Gay and Lesbian Sports Hall of Fame in 2013, and the next year, *Back on Board*, a documentary about Louganis's life, was released.

## MOVING INTO A NEW CENTURY

Professional women's golfer Muffin Spencer-Devlin came out in a 1996 article in *Sports Illustrated*. She was the first professional golfer to do so. Jim Ritts, the commissioner of the Ladies Professional Golf Association (LPGA) at the time, commented that "I don't think I'm naive, but I don't have any concerns about this. I know there are still individuals who have problems with diversity, but we've come so far as a society that I don't see this as a topic that really moves people."

As the country moved toward a new century, attitudes toward gays and lesbians were shifting dramatically in the United States.

HIV and AIDS had forced the discussion of homosexuality into every American living room. Public policies changed over the decades, with antidiscrimination legislation passing in many states. Gay couples slowly began to win state-level challenges to the right to marry, beginning with *Baehr v. Miike*, decided in 1993. The US Supreme Court's 2003 ruling in *Lawrence v. Texas* made same-sex consensual sexual activity legal in all fifty states, defeating many state and local laws that criminalized homosexual activity. Discussions of sexual identity increasingly became part of mainstream culture, with popular television shows such as *Ellen* and *Will and Grace* featuring gays and lesbians as important characters.

In fact, Ellen DeGeneres—the star of *Ellen*—was the first openly gay actor to portray a gay character on a successful prime-time television show.

Along with these shifts, attitudes toward LGBTQ+ players began to loosen up. Darren Young, a wrestler with World Wrestling Entertainment (WWE), came out casually to a reporter in an impromptu interview at an airport in 2013. After Young came out, the WWE released this statement in his support: "WWE is proud of Darren Young for being open about his sexuality, and we will continue to support him as a WWE Superstar."

WWE wrestler Darren Young *(front)* leaves the NBC *Today Show* after doing an exclusive sitdown interview about coming out as a gay man with the show's cohost Matt Lauer in August 2013.

## ATHLETE ALLY

When wrestler Hudson Taylor, who is straight, was in high school and college, he noticed the use of homophobic language and demeaning humor in sports, and it bothered him. After a very successful wrestling career at the University of Maryland, he decided to form Athlete Ally in 2011. The organization is dedicated to supporting LGBTQ+ athletes at all levels. It has professional athlete ambassadors in many sports (tennis, football, baseball, and soccer, to name a few) who lead trainings about how to combat homophobia and transphobia. These messages are aimed at fellow players, team organizations, and fans. The organization also has a program of volunteer athlete ambassadors who visit high school and college campuses to provide educational programs about how to be LGBTQ+ allies. To find out more about the organization, visit www.athleteally.org. At that site, visitors can sign a pledge to support LGBTQ+ athletes.

Wrestling coach Hudson Taylor is the founder of Athlete Ally. Hudson was a three-time NCAA All-American and two-time NCAA Academic All-American wrestler. He is a vocal advocate for LGBTQ+ rights.

Retired professional wrestler Pat Patterson, a WWE legend, came out in 2014 to a table full of other legendary wrestlers during the final episode of the reality TV show *Legends' House*. By the end of the segment, the other wrestlers' support was obvious—emotions were high, and tears, hugs, and declarations of love and support were part of the scene.

According to *Outsports*, 77 people involved in the sports world came out in 2013. And 109 players, coaches, sports administrators, and sports officials came out publicly in 2014. From October 2014 through October 2015, another 73 sports-related figures came out. Though the *Outsports* list of out athletes is not exhaustive, it provides a benchmark for the progress the LGBTQ+ sports community is making.

Religion and law have made progressive strides as well. In January 2015, the Public Religion Research Institute—a nonpartisan organization that conducts research into the ways religion, values, and public policy intersect—found that about three-quarters of one thousand survey takers who identified as religious said they would support a sports team that signed an openly gay athlete. While these survey numbers are small, the percentage of positive responses is high in the context of religion and policy. This public attitude shift about same-sex relationships was echoed in legal precedent later in the year. That June the US Supreme Court ruled in favor of same-sex marriage as US law.

## COLLEGE ACTION

In the twenty-first century, college athletes are leading the way in coming out—and very often, those coming-out stories are positive. In April 2014, Derrick Gordon of the University of Massachusetts Minutemen basketball team became the first gay Division I basketball player to come out while playing. The University of Massachusetts' athletic director, John McCutcheon, said, "UMass is proud to have Derrick Gordon as a member of our athletic family and to honor his courage and openness as a gay student-athlete. . . . UMass is committed to creating a welcoming climate where every student-athlete, coach and staff member can be true to themselves as they pursue their athletic, academic and professional goals."

Fifth-year walk-on Arizona Sun Devils offensive lineman Chip Sarafin came out publicly in August 2014, before the beginning of his senior year at Arizona State University (ASU). He said some of his teammates knew he was gay for a year before he came out. ASU running back DJ Foster said, "He knows that we have his back no matter what. . . . I'm so happy for him that he had the opportunity to [come out]." Sarafin's Sun Devils coach Todd Graham said this: "We're all about relationships built on respect, and that's respecting each other's differences whether it be cultural, religious beliefs or whatever. . . . To be real honest with you [for] our guys [Sarafin's gay identity is] not an issue."

And in January 2015, Pennsylvania's Villanova University swim team member Ryan Murtha came out to his team after a practice. Everyone clapped. Then the team went out for a traditional after-practice meal.

Not all colleges are as supportive, however. Drew Davis and Juan Varona were out volleyball players at Erskine College, a small, private religious school in South Carolina. When they came out in 2013, their teammates were accepting, and the team went on to have a strong, winning season, earning them a spot in the National Collegiate Athletic Association (NCAA) tournament. Yet two years later, in 2015, Erskine College released a statement on human

In 2014, with the support of his coach Derek Kellogg, Derrick Gordon came out as a gay man to his teammates on the University of Massachusetts Minutemen basketball team. Gordon's mother has said that in coming out, her son is finally free.

sexuality describing same-sex relationships as sinful and contrary to biblical teachings. Varona replied through an article on the *Outsports* site: "The release of this statement makes me disappointed because I have never received anything but kind treatment from everyone at this school, and my sexual orientation is no secret. So it took me by surprise. . . . [W]hen I saw the mention of sexual orientation being an issue, it just made me sad and worried for other gay people who might be struggling with confidence to come out."

# #PROUDTOPLAY

#ProudToPlay is a YouTube campaign and a Twitter hashtag launched in 2014 during the nationally recognized Pride month of June to support LGBTQ+ people in the world of sports. On the official YouTube #ProudToPlay blog, YouTube explains some of the reasons for starting the campaign:

*From the Sochi Olympics [in Russia in 2014] to the recent NFL draft, this year [2014] has seen a growing, global conversation about the lesbian, gay, bisexual, and transgender (LGBT) community in the world of sports. Many LGBT athletes are sharing their stories on YouTube, and the support they're getting from teammates and fans has helped others find the courage to do the same.*

*Sports bring together people from all backgrounds and experiences through a shared passion, and YouTube shares that spirit of connecting diverse communities to make a difference. In celebration of the [2014] World Cup in Brazil and LGBT Pride month, we're honoring the LGBT athletes, their supporters, as well as the YouTube creators who stand up for diversity in sports and elsewhere—all of whom help create an equal and inclusive playing field for everyone. Inspired by #ProudToLove last year, we're calling this effort #ProudToPlay.*

*We applaud the courage and openness of athletes at all levels who have come out and admire their teammates, friends, families, and supporters who are all proving that it doesn't matter who you are or who you love—what matters is that you put forward your best effort. We stand with our community in the belief that youth everywhere should all have the same opportunities to grow up and pursue their dreams and passions, on or off the field.*

Derek Schell, a basketball player at Hillsdale College—a conservative college in south central Michigan—came out in 2013. With his announcement, he became the first openly gay NCAA Division II basketball player. As a practicing Christian, he says he struggled with claiming his sexual identity. Like some other gay men, he turned to sports to feel more confident in his masculinity. But he also faced homophobia and hurtful comments as he was growing up in a suburb outside of Milwaukee, Wisconsin, where he attended a Catholic high school. In college he found the confidence and strength to come out and has been greeted with support from friends and other people to whom he is close. From his own experience, he urges other LGBTQ+ players to be true to themselves. He says,

> Sometimes the darkest times in life are only doorways to the best moments of your life, the ones you were meant to experience and live to see. I wanted to [come out] so that the generations to follow have an example; so that the younger LGBT youth who live afraid of who they are becoming can know they have nothing to fear and they are perfect the way they are. . . . You can be who you are and still be an athlete. You can do all the things you want to do and live a beautiful life that you've imagined for yourself. Find your peace of mind knowing you are giving your best self to the world. Be brave. Be love. But most of all, be you.

Gabrielle Ludwig *(center)* played basketball for the Mission College women's team in Santa Clara, California, from 2012 through 2014. She had the full support of her coach Corey Cafferata *(left)*, who helped her face down ugly insults and other verbal abuse at games. She is now the assistant women's basketball coach at Mission College.

# CHAPTER THREE

# ATHLETE BODIES, ATHLETE GENDERS

Gabrielle Ludwig is the first basketball player to compete at the college level in both genders. She played one year in the 1980s at Nassau (New York) Community College in the gender she was assigned at birth (male). After more than thirty years off the court, she resumed her career at Mission College in Santa Clara, California—after transitioning to female.

Ludwig has always played for the love of the game, as do all athletes. Donna Rose, a transgender woman freestyle wrestler, agrees with this truth, "We [transgender athletes] compete for the same reasons that others do: Because we love our sport, because we are athletes and because we want to continue doing something we enjoy. Competition is a fundamental right that we refuse to relinquish simply because our path to manhood or womanhood was nontraditional."

Lesbian, gay, bisexual, and queer athletes face discrimination and prejudice because of their sexuality. But nobody suggests looking in their athletic shorts to verify their anatomical sex. For transgender and intersex athletes, however, this is exactly what happens—and it starts at birth. In the United States, a doctor assigns every human a sex at birth, usually based on the baby's genitals the doctor sees at delivery. For many humans, the sex the doctor assigns matches the gender that the individual's brain tells them they are. If this is the case, the individual is considered to be cisgender. (The Latin prefix *cis* means "on the same side.")

But for transgender people (the Latin prefix *trans* means "across," "beyond," or "through"), the sex they are assigned at birth is at odds with the gender their brain tells them they are. Some transgender people choose to have medical intervention—hormone replacement therapy, surgeries, or both—to align their bodies with their gender identity. Others do not.

Intersex individuals are people who have a combination of male and female internal or external sex organs, or secondary sex characteristics (breasts, body hair patterns, and so forth) that may or may not align with their gender identity. In the past, doctors would make a choice about the sex of an intersex individual at birth and would decide what, if any, medical intervention to pursue. In the twenty-first century, however, doctors are increasingly leaving the medical intervention decision to intersex individuals and their families. Sometimes individuals who are intersex choose to have medical intervention to make their bodies align with their brain, sometimes they do not.

Discrimination against transgender and intersex athletes is common in the sporting world. This discrimination often takes the form of requiring athletes to prove their gender identity to the teams for which they want to play. These athletes may have to undergo a medical or genetic examination to verify that they have the anatomical parts that match their gender identity. In many cases, they do. But in others, a transgender or intersex athlete may not have access to medical intervention or may not have chosen to seek it. Should that athlete be excluded from playing with teammates of the gender with which that player identifies, regardless of anatomy? That question faces transgender and intersex athletes, from elementary school to the Olympics.

## COMPETITIVE ADVANTAGE

When examining the high school sports guidelines for states with conservative policies regarding transgender students, researcher Pat Griffin identified four main barriers transgender athletes face when claiming their identities and working to participate in the sports

## TRUST

If the doctor who delivers a baby labels that baby female when she's born (and places an *F* on her birth certificate) and if that person feels like a girl as she grows into a woman, then that person might not think much about her gender identity. But if someone feels conflicted because their gender identity doesn't match their body, or if a person's perception of themselves doesn't match up to society's perception of the gender binary, then that person may think about their identity a lot, especially their gender identity. Society only gives us two genders to work with—male or female. Social norms also tell us our gender should always align with the gender label we were given at birth. Yet this is not so for many transgender and gender-nonconforming people.

Sharing one's feelings about one's sense of being mismatched can be frightening, stressful, and frustrating. Rejection is almost always a possibility. Alex Jackson Nelson is a counselor and licensed social worker who works with transgender and gender nonconforming youth. Nelson talks about the importance of trusting a person's understanding of their gender identity. He says,

> *It takes courage for people to name their true gender identity or to admit that they are struggling to figure it out. When they do tell us, it's important that we believe them, even if we don't understand. It's imperative that we respect one another in all of our intersecting and varied identities.*
>
> *As a culture, we need to get better at saying to transgender individuals—no matter what body parts they do and don't have, no matter what they look like on the outside—"Your identity is important to me, and I trust you when you tell me who you are." A transgender identity is a valid identity we must trust and acknowledge, even if we don't know the full scientific explanation for why it happens. In the sports world, it will be an enormous leap to make that change, given that teams and locker rooms are segregated by sex and gender. But it's an important change to make.*

they love. First, many people believe transgender girls (women who were assigned male at birth but who identify as female) are really boys because of their genitals, despite their affirmed gender identity as a girl. Second, Griffin has identified a fear that cisgender boys (boys who are born anatomically male and who identify as male) will pretend to be girls to be able to win in girls' championships.

These boys might also pretend to be girls to get more playing time on girls' teams if they're not top-flight players on the boys' teams. This thinking is based on the stereotype that boys are better athletes than girls and that it's easy for boys to beat girls. (For this reason, fears that cisgender girls would pretend to be boys to compete on boys' teams are not common.) Third, Griffin found a misperception that transgender girls pose a safety risk for cisgender girls in high-contact sports, such as basketball and field hockey, because they are assumed to be physically stronger or larger than players assigned female at birth. Fourth, she found a concern that transgender girls have a competitive advantage over cisgender girls because they were identified as and socialized as boys.

Griffin and other experts maintain that these barriers to athletic participation are grounded in stereotypes reinforced by individuals with little or no knowledge of what it means to be transgender. To date, no transgender or intersex women athletes have actually dominated competitions in their chosen sports. These athletes compete and perform as all other athletes do—with victories and defeats.

Experts point out that the physical characteristics of any player will depend on the player's conditioning and skill levels, not on their genetic makeup. Trans and intersex athletes, therefore, have no inherent advantage over other players. And players are at risk from other players who are stronger, faster, and more skilled than they are, no matter what sex chromosomes they have. Competitive advantage can also be driven by other factors. Swimmer Michael Phelps, for instance, has very long arms that help him move through the water faster. In addition, one athlete may have a stronger, more ferocious competitive drive than another, translating into a determination to win.

## GENDER VERIFICATION

In the twenty-first century, sports officials still have the right to require female athletes to undergo verification tests if that athlete's gender is in question. Gender verification testing can involve gynecologists, endocrinologists (doctors who deal with hormones), psychologists, and internal medicine specialists. Caster Semenya is an intersex middle distance runner from South Africa who officials suspected has high levels of testosterone for a woman (a condition called hyperandrogenism). The International Association of Athletics Federations (IAAF) required her to be tested in 2009 to clarify her gender. No one is sure exactly what happened to Semenya after she was tested. It's possible she was asked to take hormone regulators to control her high testosterone levels and bring them closer to more typical women's levels. Semenya hasn't spoken about it. But she has never run as fast as she did before her testing.

Dutee Chand, a sprinter from India, also was tested and found to have hyperandrogenism, and the IAAF barred her from competing in 2014. But the Court of Arbitration for Sport (CAS), based in Switzerland, overturned the IAAF's ruling and gave her back the right to compete in 2015. The ruling also asked the IAAF to do more research to prove that higher levels of natural testosterone (not ingested from another source) give women a competitive advantage. The CAS also said that "it remain[s] inappropriate to subject athletes to sex verification, external genitalia

Intersex runner Caster Semenya was required to undergo gender verification testing in 2009. She went on to compete as a woman, winning a gold medal in the women's 800-meter run at the 2009 World Championships. She also won silver medals at the 2011 World Championships and the 2012 Summer Olympics, both in the 800-meter run. In 2015 she married runner Violet Raseboya.

examinations or chromosome testing." In the ruling, the court said, "Although athletics events are divided into discrete male and female categories, sex in humans is not simply binary [either male or female]. . . . Nature is not neat. There is no single determinant of sex."

Many people wonder if these test requirements are fair, especially since males are typically not required to undergo gender testing. In addition, an individual's hormone levels can fluctuate based on something as simple as the time of day, so no gender testing method is 100 percent accurate.

Rebecca Jordan-Young, a professor of gender and sexuality studies, and Katrina Karkazis, a research scholar in biomedical ethics, aren't sure what the best methods are for ensuring equity and level playing fields in sports for transgender and intersex competitors. Using only genetic markers (and disregarding self-identification) isn't as helpful as organizations such as the IAAF would like. Jordan-Young and Karkazis suggest instead,

> *What about letting go of the idea that the ultimate goal of a fair policy is to protect the "purity" of women's competitions? If the goal is instead to group athletes so that everyone has a chance to play, to excel and—yes—to win, then sex-segregated competition is just one of many possible options, and in many cases it might not be the best one.*
>
> *Sex segregation may obscure other gender inequities in sports. Men, for example, have forty more events in the Olympics and have longer distances and durations—with no clear rationale.*
>
> *Sex segregation is probably a good idea in some sports, at some levels and at some moments. But it is time to refocus policy discussions at every level so that sex segregation is one means to achieve fairness, not the ultimate goal. Ensuring gender equity through access to opportunity is just as important.*

## SCHUYLER BAILAR

In June 2015, Schuyler Bailar became the first transgender swimmer in the history of Division 1 intercollegiate athletics. Bailar is a trans man who swims for the Harvard University men's team. When he was living as a woman, he had been offered a scholarship to swim on Harvard's women's team. He accepted and decided to postpone some of his medical transition so he could keep his scholarship with the women's team.

Before his freshman year at Harvard started in fall 2015, however, Bailar had decided to make his trans identity official—and public. In February 2015, Bailar received a life-changing phone call from the Harvard women's swim coach. She told Bailar that if he chose to, he could swim for the men's team instead. After visiting the campus to meet with both teams, Bailar chose to swim for the Harvard men's team, aligning his athletic affiliation with his true gender.

Schuyler Bailar, a swimmer on Harvard University's men's team, has openly shared his transition process on social media. He has hope for the future and encourages other trans athletes to come out and share their gender identity.

## "A RELUCTANT PIONEER"

The first documented transgender and intersex athletes date to the early twentieth century. Mark Weston, competing as a female before his transition, was a national champion English shot-putter and javelin thrower in the 1920s. He transitioned to male in the mid-1930s and left competitive sports. In the same era, Zdeněk Koubek—assigned female at birth in Czechoslovakia—held a women's world record in the 800-meter run. He gave up a potential coaching career to have gender confirmation surgery in the mid-1930s.

Fast-forward to the 1970s and to American tennis player Renée Richards. She was born in New York in 1934, and she had always been a strong tennis player. She had played in college and had a promising amateur career before her transition in 1975, after which she began playing in local tournaments for women. After some wins, a television reporter outed her, and controversy erupted.

In some cases, female tennis competitors withdrew from competitions in which Richards was enrolled because they believed she had an unfair physical advantage, having the musculature and height of a man. Additionally, when Richards applied to play in the 1976 US Open tennis tournament, the United States Tennis Association (USTA) denied Richards's entry, citing a never-before-implemented women-born-women policy. Richards refused to take the Barr body test, a chromosomal test to determine biological sex, and one of the tests used for gender testing at that time by the International Olympic Committee and other sports organizations. Richards was subsequently barred from all USTA events. The Wimbledon and Italian Open also barred Richards for that year. As a result, Richards sued the USTA in 1976 for her right to play tennis as a woman. The next year, she won the case and a court order admitting her to the 1977 US Open. Judge Alfred M. Ascione, who heard the case in New York state court, found in Richards's favor. He said requiring Richards to pass the Barr body test was "grossly unfair,

discriminatory and inequitable, and a violation of her rights."

Richards's tennis career ended in 1981 when she retired. She worked as an ophthalmologist in her own practice and went on to coach other tennis players, including Martina Navratilova in two of her Wimbledon wins. In 2015, reflecting back on her life as a pioneer in the transgender sports world, Richards said, "I was a reluctant pioneer, so I can't take that much credit for it. I was not an activist. It was a private act for my own self-betterment, for what I wanted to do. I wanted to go and play tennis, you know? And I wanted to stand up and say what I was."

## FALLON FOX

Ohio-born mixed martial arts (MMA) fighter Fallon Fox transitioned from male to female long before she began fighting professionally, but she was not out as transgender when she began her MMA career. After a reporter dropped hints to Fox privately that he knew she had transitioned, Fox outed herself in an interview in March 2013, becoming the first openly transgender athlete in MMA history. Fox was unprepared for the reaction to her news. She remembers, "The scope of anger and vitriol [nasty criticism] that I received initially . . . That was disheartening, tragic. It was mind-blowing."

Competitors such as Ronda Rousey, the bantamweight Ultimate Fighting Championship fighter, refused to fight Fox, claiming that Fox had an unfair physical advantage. Experts point out that Fox may actually be at a disadvantage. Testosterone is one of the contributors to strength and stamina in both men and women, but because she was born a man and medically transitioned to female, Fox has very little testosterone in her body. This deficit happens when men who transition to female choose hormone replacement therapy to replace the male hormone testosterone with the female hormone estrogen. They also often choose to medically remove their testes, which release testosterone. Cisgender women produce only small amounts of testosterone each day, and if transgender women do not have testes, their testosterone levels are dramatically lowered. With miniscule amounts of testosterone in her body, Fox is therefore theoretically at a biological disadvantage. It is her training and skill that make her a formidable fighter, not her biological level of testosterone.

The controversy about Fox's perceived advantage played out in

the media. In March 2013, shortly after Fox came out, MMA commentator and comedian Joe Rogan publicly targeted Fox, claiming she had an unfair fighting advantage because she was born a man. In November 2014, an article about transgender athletes in *Vice* criticized Rogan for his comments. Rogan struck back with more claims of unfair advantage. Fox refuted his arguments in three blog posts, offering scientific evidence to discredit Rogan's claims.

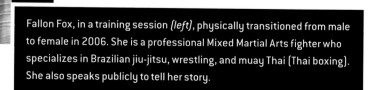

Fallon Fox, in a training session *(left)*, physically transitioned from male to female in 2006. She is a professional Mixed Martial Arts fighter who specializes in Brazilian jiu-jitsu, wrestling, and muay Thai (Thai boxing). She also speaks publicly to tell her story.

# AMELIA GAPIN

Some transgender athletes, such as Fallon Fox or Caitlyn Jenner, gain a lot of attention. But some athletes with equally compelling stories engage in their sports without the spotlight of fame. Amelia Gapin is a marathon runner and trans woman living in New Jersey. In fall 2015, she competed to have her photo on the cover of *Women's Running* magazine. On *Entirely Amelia* (www.entirelyamelia.com), she writes about her life as a trans woman and athlete. Gapin's stories demonstrate both the power of sports in an athlete's life and exactly why all athletes deserve safe spaces to be themselves.

For Gapin, running isn't just a way to keep her body healthy—running has been her lifeline to peace. When *Women's Running* asked her how running has changed her life, she said,

> *Running has literally saved my life time and time again. When I was transitioning, running was a safe place to deal with all of the things going on in my life and process both the ups and downs of it all. There is no way I would have survived transition without running. Even outside of transitioning, running has always been there for me as an escape from my depression and a way to work through everything so I could move past it. It's brought me peace and bliss when I most needed it. I've started runs feeling on the verge of suicide and by the end had a huge smile on my face and saw nothing but the beauty in the world. I wouldn't still be here if I didn't have running in my life.*

Gapin is a private person, and being on the cover of a major magazine doesn't appeal to her—she doesn't want or need the personal attention. However, she knows the possibility of a cover spot can be considered a victory. She says,

> *For a women's running magazine to put a transgender woman on their cover means they're willing to take the stance that trans women count the same as cis women in athletics, or at least running. They can't put a transgender woman on their cover and then say she's not a woman. This is really big to me. Of course, a magazine cover doesn't instantly change the world, but Women's Running is a major running magazine and having a transgender woman on the cover would still be pretty rad and, at the least, makes a statement.*

Speaking in defense of Fox was Dr. Eric Vilain, MD, PhD, a genetic researcher at the University of California at Los Angeles. In the *Vice* article, he wrote, "Research suggests that androgen deprivation [blocking the hormone testosterone] and cross sex hormone treatment in male-to-female transsexuals reduces muscle mass. . . . Accordingly, one year of hormone therapy is an appropriate transitional time before a male-to-female student-athlete competes on a women's team." Fox met these criteria. But Rogan has not backed off his claims. One twist to the story is that MMA fighter Ashlee Evans-Smith, who defeated Fox in 2013 (while claiming Fox had an unfair advantage), was banned from the sport for nine months in 2015. Evans-Smith tested positive for doping. She had been using the diuretic hydrochlorothiazide, a substance that causes a person to urinate frequently. It helps athletes lose water weight and can potentially mask other banned substances by excreting them faster from the body. Its use gives athletes an unfair advantage.

## KYE ALLUMS

Kye Allums identifies as an artist, an athlete, and a transgender man. Assigned female at birth in Florida in 1989, Allums came out as transgender in 2010 while playing basketball for the George Washington University women's team, in Washington, DC. It was not easy to come out while playing for a university, Allums said. He described what it felt like to inhabit his body before transitioning, when he suffered from gender dysphoria (very intense discomfort and distress experienced by people who feel a mismatch between the sex assigned to them at birth and their gender identity):

*It's like being sick. It's like having the flu. It's like you want to rip the skin off of your body. It's the most uncomfortable, unbearable feeling in the world. I could not focus on basketball feeling like that. All I wanted to do was escape my body and run away. . . . To bring that focus back to basketball, I needed to hear male pronouns. . . . Some people would tell me that I was not a guy, or that I was confused. Everyone is entitled to their own opinion. I know who I am.*

Allums is a vocal advocate for LGBTQ+ issues, but his journey to accepting his role as a public voice was stressful. After Allums came out, ESPN released an episode in 2011 of *Outside the Lines*, a show that looks at sports issues off the field. The episode focused on Allums and his transition. The film included information and childhood photos that Allums's mother had shared with the ESPN crew. Allums asked ESPN not to share that information with the world—he was not interested in the world knowing his previous name and seeing his childhood photos. ESPN aired it anyway. Allums later said that the exposure of his previous life left him feeling suicidal. In response to the ESPN episode, Allums deactivated his social media accounts to protect his privacy. A year later, when he chose to reengage in social media, he discovered messages from despairing trans individuals who expressed to him their intent to commit suicide because of the pressures of being trans in an unwelcoming world. Allums responded to the suicidal individuals, offering support and comfort. The experience left a deep impact and set him on a course of LGBT activism. In 2013 he commented about his decision to be a public voice of advocacy:

> Right then and there (more or less), I decided I should share that message [of trans acceptance] with other kids, too. I started by reaching out to every LGBT organization in the country. At first, only colleges invited me to speak. Recently, however, high schools have asked as well. It makes me feel good to visit a high school in a conservative part of Florida—an area where LGBT students are typically harassed—and get people to understand how to become more tolerant. I save a lot of time for questions because I want people to ask me ignorant questions—questions they don't even know how to ask—so I can teach them how to respectfully interact with a trans person whom they might meet later in life.

## CAITLYN JENNER

Caitlyn Jenner's story marks one of the most high-profile gender transitions in the twenty-first-century world of athletics. Assigned male at birth in 1949 in Mount Kisco, New York, Caitlyn was a champion water skier in high school and a popular athlete. Sports kept Jenner's gender dysphoria at bay. Jenner says simply, "Sports saved my life." Jenner also performed well in high school track-and-field meets and went to college on a football scholarship. Jenner went on to win the 1976 Olympic gold medal in the men's decathlon, a ten-event competition and one of the most demanding sports an athlete can endure. The Olympic decathlon is composed of ten individual sports: the 100-meter dash, the long jump, the

shot put, the high jump, the 400-meter dash, the 110-meter hurdles, the discus throw, the pole vault, the javelin throw, and the 1,500-meter dash. Jenner had placed tenth in the sport in the 1972 Olympics but grabbed the world's attention with a stunning performance four years later. Whether people were sports fans or not, most Americans knew about Jenner's triumph. That year was the bicentennial of the birth of the United States, and with Jenner's gold medal, an American had won one of the most intense athletic accomplishments in the world.

As a result of Jenner's Olympic glory, Jenner gained several lucrative endorsement deals—inclvuding appearing on the front of a Wheaties cereal box in 1977, a marketing strategy reserved for the nation's top athletes. Jenner also had minor roles on television and in films. Unbeknownst to everyone except Jenner's immediate family, Jenner began her gender transition in the late 1980s, putting it on hold around 1990. After that, Jenner was in and out of the spotlight, most notably through a marriage to Kris Kardashian and through the couple's participation in the reality television show *Keeping Up with the Kardashians*, which debuted in 2007. After

## CHRIS MOSIER

Chris Mosier is a transgender Ironman triathlete. Triathletes compete in three sports: swimming, running, and cycling. Mosier began competing in triathlons in 2009 as a woman and then began to compete as a man in 2010 as he started his transition. As a trans man, Mosier felt a need to see himself reflected in the sports world around him, and he wanted that for other trans athletes as well. He says, "As an athlete, I did not know of any other trans male athletes who transitioned and were competing at a high level, and that is what I wanted for myself. I don't want any other person—particularly a young person—to be able to say that."

Mosier went on to start two websites: GO! Athletes, a support network for current and former high school and college LGBTQ+ athletes, and Trans*Athlete, a comprehensive resource dedicated to transgender inclusion at all levels of athletic competition. In June 2015, Mosier won a spot on Team USA's national men's duathlon (run, bike, run) team. He became the first transgender athlete to win a spot on a US national team that matches his true gender identity, rather than his identity assigned at birth. Mosier wants to be an inspiration to others as much as he wants to be an elite athlete. He says, "My hope is that athletes who are questioning their gender identity can see me and hear my story and know they don't have to give up their identity as an athlete to live authentically."

splitting from Kardashian in 2013, Jenner publicly acknowledged her transition in April 2015 with a two-hour television interview with journalist Diane Sawyer. Two months later, in June 2015, *Vanity Fair* magazine published a front-cover coming-out article, introducing the world to Caitlyn Jenner through an in-depth interview and a glamorous photo spread. Jenner received intense media scrutiny—both praise and criticism—for her very public announcement.

Some people point to Jenner's coming out as a watershed moment in public acceptance for transgender individuals. In July 2015, Caitlyn Jenner received the Arthur Ashe Courage Award. Choosing Jenner for the award was both applauded and disparaged.

Nonetheless, her acceptance speech at the awards ceremony that month was a poignant and timely call for acceptance for all. Jenner said,

> For the people out there wondering what this is all about—whether it's about courage or controversy or publicity. . . . I'll tell you what it's all about. It's about what happens from here. It's not just about one person, it's about thousands of people. It's not just about me, it's about all of us accepting one another. We're all different. That's not a bad thing, that's a good thing and while it may not be easy to get past the things you always don't understand, I want to prove that it is absolutely possible if we only do it together.

Australian swimmer and Olympic medalist Ian Thorpe came out as a gay man in 2014. He had publicly denied his homosexuality for years, saying that the lie eventually became too big to refute. He points out that in the end, "I felt like I'd betrayed people by being dishonest about [being gay]."

# CHAPTER FOUR

# THE GATEKEEPERS

Various governing bodies regulate the rules of play, eligibility, and other standards for competitive sports at amateur and professional levels. The organizations vary at the local, regional, national, and international levels. These governing bodies do not necessarily collaborate for consistent rules and regulations related to LGBTQ+ policy. Issues are often approached from differing points of view. For example, Michael Sam had protection as a player in the NFL. The league has a nondiscrimination clause adopted in 2011 that includes sexual orientation. The NFL also has a personal conduct policy that punishes abuse or harassment of other players. MLB has a similar nondiscrimination clause adopted in 2011, as do Major League Soccer, adopted in 2004, and the National Basketball Association, adopted in 2011.

Hockey—the sport many people consider to be the roughest and least progressive—has taken a strong official stance to support LGBTQ+ players. In 2013 the National Hockey League and the NHL Players' Association partnered with You Can Play, an organization that fights homophobia in sports. According to NHL commissioner Gary Bettman, "The official policy of the NHL is one of inclusion on the ice, in our locker rooms and in the stands." And You Can Play helps the NHL provide that inclusion. The partnership provides education on LGBTQ+ issues to players and coaches as well as to media and fans. The following is the official mission statement of You Can Play:

> *You Can Play works to insure the safety and inclusion of all in sports—including LGBT athletes, coaches and fans.*

*You Can Play works to guarantee that athletes are given a fair opportunity to compete, judged by other athletes and fans alike, only by what they contribute to the sport or their team's success.*

*You Can Play seeks to challenge the culture of locker rooms and spectator areas by focusing only on an athlete's skills, work ethic and competitive spirit.*

Philadelphia Flyers hockey scout Patrick Burke launched You Can Play in 2012 after the death of his brother Brendan Burke in a 2010 car accident. Brendan Burke had been a student manager for the Miami University RedHawks team in Ohio. He came out in 2009 with support from their father, Brian, then the general manager of the Toronto Maple Leafs. Brendan Burke wanted to tell

his story to show that the world of hockey supported LGBTQ+ players and coaches. Patrick Burke remembered his brother after his death with an article in *Outsports*. He said,

*All it takes is one person to personalize and humanize homosexuality, which remains, unfortunately, an abstract concept to most athletes. Our family experienced this when Brendan made his courageous*

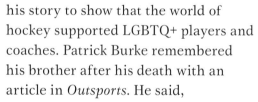

Patrick Burke *(left)*, founder of You Can Play, says that the NHL is ready to welcome and support gay players who come out. But he says he knows that the pressure to remain in the closet and the potential for negative backlash after coming out are still powerful factors that keep gay NHL players from going public.

*announcement. I experienced it, personally, when Brendan told me he was gay. Suddenly I was aware of the impact of my words, of the pains adolescent gays experience in the locker room, and of the complete irrelevance of sexual orientation when evaluating someone's character. . . . In the wake of Brendan's death, our family has vowed to continue the fight for equality in sports.*

You Can Play is the labor of love Patrick Burke created to continue the fight. You Can Play offers inclusion education to men's and women's sports of all kinds, from college to professional teams, in the United States and in Canada.

## INTERNATIONAL OLYMPIC COMMITTEE

The International Olympic Committee is one of the most well-known governing bodies in sports. In 2004 the IOC adopted the Stockholm consensus (created in Stockholm, Sweden, in 2003), a formal policy outlining the rules of participation for transgender athletes. These rules state that to compete in the Olympic Games, transgender athletes must have undergone at least two years of cross-sex hormone treatment prior to competition, be legally recognized as their gender by government agencies (through government-issued identity documents) in their country, and have had gender confirmation surgery. These rules aren't perfect, since not all transgender athletes have access to or choose to access these procedures. However, the Stockholm consensus was an important step toward recognizing transgender athletes in Olympic competition.

About ten years after the Stockholm consensus went into effect, Russia hosted the 2014 Winter Olympics in Sochi. Russia is a country with harsh anti-LGBTQ+ laws, and advocacy groups around the world, along with individual athletes, called for a boycott of the Games. While the United States chose not to boycott the

Games, President Barack Obama and his family did not attend. Instead, Obama appointed openly gay athletes—figure skater Brian Boitano; tennis legend Billie Jean King (who did not attend due to her mother's poor health); and Caitlin Cahow, an Olympic medalist in women's hockey—as part of the US delegation to the Games. After Sochi the IOC expanded its Sixth Fundamental Principle of Olympism (the IOC's antidiscrimination principle) to specifically include sexual orientation. This change may prevent countries with discriminatory LGBTQ+ laws and practices from hosting future Olympic Games, although critics wish the IOC had been more explicit about the limitations that could be imposed upon these host countries. Critics also feel the expanded principle did not go far enough. It does not cover gender identity and gender expression as part of the principle.

In January 2016, the IOC released some rule changes they intend to make regarding transgender athletes. The changes will be made before the 2016 Olympics. The new rules remove the requirement of gender reassignment surgery for a transgender athlete and allow transgender women to compete after only one year of hormone replacement therapy. These rules align with the NCAA guidelines for transgender athletes.

In 2009 President Barack Obama (right) awarded Billie Jean King (left) the Presidential Medal of Freedom for her work on behalf of fairness and justice for women and LGBTQ+ peoples in the world of sports. She is the first female athlete—and the first open lesbian—to receive the distinguished honor.

## NATIONAL COLLEGIATE ATHLETIC ASSOCIATION

The most important rule-making body for college sports is the National Collegiate Athletic Association. The organization has extensive antidiscrimination policies and supports LGBTQ+ inclusion at all levels and in all sports. For this reason, college athletes are more likely to be out than professional athletes. The following is the NCAA statement about LGBTQ+ athletes, coaches, and staff:

> *The NCAA association-wide subcommittee for LGBTQ inclusion understands that LGBTQ student-athletes, coaches, and administrators too often endure social stigma and emotional trauma on the court, in the classroom, and in the workplace, which serves as a bar to fair and equitable competitive and learning environments.*
>
> *We celebrate the courage and fortitude of student-athletes, coaches and administrators who have bravely revealed their sexual identities to teammates, colleagues, and their entire communities.*
>
> *Furthermore, we take tremendous pride in the support of all lesbian, gay, bisexual, transgender and questioning (LGBTQ) individuals, especially those associated with the organization, member institutions, and affiliates.*

How do we know these policies work? Schuyler Bailar is an incredible success story: he didn't lose his Harvard swimming scholarship after he came out as a trans man. NCAA policies provided him with the freedom to make his choice to be out and to compete on the men's swim team. Those same policies also supported his coaches in welcoming him and making him comfortable on the team.

## K–12 POLICIES

At the K–12 level of sports, policies to protect LGBTQ+ athletes vary from state to state and school district to school district. Some states have no policy; some states have partially inclusive policies; and some states have inclusive, protective policies for LGBTQ+ students. Very often the debates about these policies can be divisive and discriminatory, particularly regarding transgender issues. For example, in 2015 in Elko, Nevada, a transgender boy asked to use the boys' locker room in his middle school. The school board rejected his request. A South Dakota lawmaker suggested inspection of players' genitals as the determining factor for deciding whether that player should compete on a boys' or a girls' team. But states such as New York are working toward what many people feel is a more sensible, fairer approach—a student can produce a note from a parent or health professional to confirm the student's gender identity.

Sometimes a state's K–12 policies can be stricter than the policies of a larger organization such as the NCAA. For example, Indiana's transgender policies require that a transgender student have gender reassignment surgery to compete on the team that fits the person's self-identified gender. The NCAA only requires that same athlete

## LGBT SPORTS SUMMIT

Since 2012 the LGBT Sports Summit has been held in Portland, Oregon. The event, sponsored by Nike, brings together coaches, athletes, and sports advocates to discuss wide-ranging information about LGBTQ+ involvement in sports. In 2015 the summit hosted 120 individuals. Attendees participated in panels on topics such as how to take care of yourself after coming out and how to create trans-inclusive policies for a sports team. Attendees are also asked to create an implementation plan for a project in their local community. The goal of these plans is to spread LGBTQ+ athlete acceptance in the wider world.

In 2012 Pat Griffin said, "This summit happened at the right time. . . . We are riding the crest of a wave of attitude change about LGBTQ people in sports. We hope that the action plans that were identified at the summit will speed up this change."

to be participating in hormone therapy. These stricter state policies can make it difficult for some transgender students to participate in sports. And these policies are in effect while student-athletes would be developing key skills to compete at higher levels of competition later on, possibly derailing an athlete's chances for future competitive play and success.

## TRANSGENDER ATHLETES IN MINNESOTA

In 2014 the Minnesota State High School League (MSHSL), in response to guidance from the National Federation of State High School Associations, decided to craft a policy to support transgender student-athletes. As the league drafted its policy and asked for public commentary, many individuals and groups sent feedback. One group, the Child Protection League Action did not support the policy and began placing ads in various Minnesota newspapers to persuade parents that transgender students posed a risk to cisgender students. The ads included inflammatory messaging about the policy, including "The end of girls' sports?" and "Her dreams of a scholarship shattered, your 14-year-old daughter just lost her position on an all-girl team to a male. . . . and now she may have to shower with him."

In December 2014, the board of the MSHSL held a public hearing to debate the new policy. The hearing was packed with individuals testifying and protesting on both sides of the issue. After hearing the wide range of viewpoints, the league's board adopted a policy to allow students to play sports on the team that reflects their lived gender, not the sex assigned to them at birth. Students must provide statements from parents or doctors confirming their gender to school officials. The students are not required to provide proof of hormone replacement therapy or gender confirmation surgery. The policy took effect in the 2015–2016 school year, making Minnesota the thirty-third state to have a policy supporting transgender athletes.

# CHILD M'S STORY

Child M is an eight-year-old athlete growing up in a small city in the Upper Midwest. Child M was assigned female at birth and is gender fluid. She has asked her parents to use "she" and "her" as her pronouns. But she feels more at home in boys' clothes and presents to the world as a boy, after declaring to her mother "I am not a girl" when she was a toddler. Child M's mother shares these thoughts about her child's athletic participation:

[My child] has played on boys' basketball teams and girls' soccer teams for the past two years. . . . In the case of soccer, the organizers were insistent that her biological gender determine her placement on a team, not her skill level or gender presentation. She has had . . . reactions to her shaved head while on the girls' team: 1) parents and other children asking if she had cancer, and 2) other coaches inquiring why a boy was playing on our team.

She left soccer this year. When she played on the boys' basketball team, she had no negative responses at all. She was referred to by male pronouns, and her teammates, who mainly know her gender, seemed to forget . . . she is an exceptionally athletic and competitive child. She seems to especially like these situations where she is able to simply be—where her gender is not an issue, and she can pass as, and live as, a boy.

In the case of her school, they have been incredibly open and supportive of her, in almost every case. The staff has even found a single stall bathroom for her so she doesn't need to make that decision [about which bathroom to use] each time she needs to use the bathroom.

We don't really know where our child's gender identification lies at this point. Although her gender presentation is wholly masculine, she is fluid in her identification, preferring gender-neutral descriptors where possible. She has a swagger none of our sons possess, but also expresses the desire to give birth. We hope that she has the opportunity to continue to play sports on the teams where she is considered an asset, and that allow her to feel part of the group's successes.

Elliott Kunerth, a transgender man and student-athlete who graduated from a Minnesota high school in 2015, saw the misleading ad from the Child Protection League Action in his local newspaper and was furious about its misinformation. He attended the MSHSL hearing in December 2014 to support the new transgender policy and spoke in front of the board. Kunerth says,

*The impact these protective policies, laws, and regulations have upon transgender youth is tremendous. Not only does the MSHSL policy allow transgender players to participate on teams that match their identities, but it spreads the education and validity that transgender men are men; transgender women are women. These policies help erase the ignorance*

Seventeen-year-old trans man Elliott Kunerth *(facing camera)* hugs girlfriend Kelsi Pettit in 2014 after the board of the MSHSL voted for a policy to allow trans athletes to participate in league-sponsored extracurricular activities.

*surrounding our community by allowing trans people to be treated equally in the world of athletics, as human beings with valid identities. Although my personal fear and hesitancy of gendered sports teams will always remain a factor in my decision to abstain [from competitive sports], I sincerely hope they are not something future transgender youth will have to experience. We are all just people. We all deserve fairness, equality, kindness and respect; a right to live the lives we know are best for us.*

## LAWS AT WORK

Along with institutional policies, laws in the United States provide a framework for legal protections for LGBTQ+ athletes. For example, Title IX—passed as part of the Education Amendments of 1972—is a federal law that declares that discrimination based on sex is illegal in federally funded educational activities and programs (including elementary, middle, and high schools). Title IX is responsible for making sure that men and women have equal access to sports at the high school and college level (though the sports might be different for each sex). Because Title IX concerns itself with outlawing sexual harassment and violence against Americans based on sex, it also protects transgender students and athletes in schools. The US Department of Education's Office for Civil Rights (OCR) says,

*Title IX's sex discrimination prohibition extends to claims of discrimination based on gender identity or failure to conform to stereotypical notions of masculinity or femininity and OCR accepts such complaints for investigation.*

If athletes have a complaint, they can file an online form with the OCR. According to the OCR's website,

*These civil rights laws extend to all state education agencies, elementary and secondary school systems, colleges and universities, vocational schools, proprietary schools, state vocational rehabilitation agencies, libraries, and museums that receive federal financial assistance from ED [the Department of Education].*

Because public schools receive federal financial assistance, any student-athlete playing at any level for any public school has access to OCR protections.

Title IX has already been used to protect a transgender student in Palatine, Illinois. In late 2015, the US Department of Education mandated that a school district there allow a transgender girl to shower with her teammates in the girls' locker room, rather than behind a curtain in a separate part of the locker room, where the district insisted she change. The OCR cited Title IX in its decision, identifying the district's insistence on separate changing facilities for the girl as sex discrimination.

The Employment Non-Discrimination Act (ENDA) is also on the horizon. Passed by the US Senate in November 2013, the law would protect LGBTQ+ individuals from hiring, firing, and other kinds of employment discrimination based on sexual orientation or gender identity, a protection that would extend to sports. ENDA has been up for a vote at various times since 1994, but 2013 was the first time the US Senate passed the bill. If the US House of Representatives passes it and the president signs it, it becomes law.

## LAWSUITS

Sometimes LGBTQ+ athletes have chosen to take their fight for the right to play into a court of law. The National Center for Lesbian Rights has helped several LGBTQ+ athletes win their discrimination cases. In December 2005, Penn State University (PSU) basketball player Jennifer Harris filed a lawsuit against PSU's very popular women's basketball coach, Rene Portland. Harris, who left the school at the end of the 2005 school year, alleged that because Portland perceived her to be a lesbian, the coach created a hostile environment for her on the team. Harris claimed that Portland hassled her, left her out of team functions, and asked her to be more feminine. At the time, Portland appeared to have a "no tolerance" policy for lesbians on the PSU team. Harris, who says she is not a lesbian, filed a federal lawsuit in which other former PSU players spoke out about Portland's harassment of them for the same reasons. The lawsuit was settled in the players' favor in February 2007, and Coach Portland chose to resign in March 2007. Terms of the settlement were not disclosed.

Mianne Bagger, a Danish woman golfer who is also transgender, fought with the Ladies Professional Golf Association (LPGA) in 2003 for the right to play as a transgender woman and lost. She

now plays on other tours in Europe and Australia. In 2010 world champion long driver Lana Lawless sued the LPGA over her right to play golf as a transgender woman. At the time, LPGA rules stated that golfers had to be female at birth to compete in LPGA tournaments. Lawless was therefore unable

For twenty-seven years, Rene Portland was the powerful and successful head coach of the Penn State women's basketball team. Portland resigned in 2007 after losing an anti-lesbian harassment lawsuit. The 2009 documentary *Training Rules* tells the story of homophobia in women's college sports, focusing on the Penn State team under Portland.

to compete. She claimed the policy violated her civil rights and cost her lost earnings. In November 2010, the LPGA voted to remove the "female at birth" requirement, and Lawless dropped her lawsuit in 2011 when she was allowed to compete.

Lawsuits also affect private companies such as CrossFit, a California-based fitness company that provides an intense strength and conditioning program along with competitive games. In March 2014, athletic trainer and CrossFit participant Chloie Jönsson, who is a trans woman, sued CrossFit for $2.5 million in damages for not allowing her to participate in the women's division of the company's CrossFit Games. According to Jönsson, she and her CrossFit team had been training for the 2013 CrossFit Games, assuming the regulations and requirements regarding transgender competitors would be the same as the IOC's—legal documents, surgery, and hormones. But CrossFit told Jönsson, who had gender confirmation surgery in 2006, that she had an unfair physical advantage over other female competitors because she had been assigned male at birth.

Jönsson said choosing to sue CrossFit wasn't an easy decision. She has a lot of support from teammates, friends, and family in choosing to sue the company. Though she has received hate mail related to her lawsuit, she chose to ignore it. Jönsson says, "While I feel more vulnerable than I ever have before, I'm no longer running from myself or anyone else. Win or lose, I'm happy to say that I'm finally able to own who I am—all of me." The case is pending resolution.

In the fall of 2015, seniors at Oak Park High School in Kansas City, Missouri, elected transgender cheerleader Landon Patterson their homecoming queen. The transphobic Westboro Baptist Church protested Patterson's coronation, but a large group of students and other allies showed up in her support. The protesters quickly disbanded.

# CHAPTER FIVE

# FUTURE PLAYS

National Coming Out Day is every October 11 in the United States. In October 2015, *Outsports* ran a feature story about seventy-three LGBTQ+ athletes who had come out since October 2014. While seventy-three people fill up a room, they're a drop in the bucket compared to the millions of Americans who play amateur and professional sports at all levels in the United States. But it's seventy-three more athletes who are living their lives openly and freely.

Landon Patterson is a transgender teen girl. Since her freshman year, she has been a cheerleader at Oak Park High School in Kansas City, Missouri. But because she was assigned male at birth, she has had to wear a boy's outfit on the squad. As of summer 2015, the Missouri State High School Activities Association allowed her to compete with the girls' team and to wear the girls' uniform. And that fall, her classmates elected her their homecoming queen.

Patterson participates in her sport for the same reasons any other athlete does. She says, "Being an athlete has put me in a group of other athletes. It gave me a second family. Being an athlete has pushed me to be a leader. It's helped me push myself, kept me in shape, made me stronger and given me an outlet."

The sports world will continue to evolve. During Major League Baseball's All-Star Break in 2014, the league announced it had created an ambassador for inclusion: Billy Bean, a former pro outfielder who came out in 1999 (after his playing career was over). He provided guidance to David Denson, the minor-league baseball player who came out in August 2015. The ambassador's role is to provide guidance and training to both major- and minor-league baseball clubs in how to support LGBTQ+ baseball players. In January 2016, Bean was promoted to the league's Vice President for Social Responsibility and Inclusion, and Curtis Pride, a former MLB outfielder, became the Ambassador for Inclusion. While not every league or organization has such a position, visible support for LGBTQ+ inclusion in one sport creates ripples in all sports. In October 2015, for example, silver Olympic medal winner Gus Kenworthy, a freestyle skier, came out. His sport is all action and flash, with lots of masculine posturing. Kenworthy worried about the possibility of a negative reaction to his announcement. But his organization, the United States Ski and Snowboard Association (USSA), was happy to support him. USSA president Tiger Shaw said, "We admire Gus for having the strength to tell the world who he is as a person, and paving the way for others to do the same."

While the sports world moves forward, it is also reaching back to honor the LGBTQ+ heroes who were out before their sport was

ready to accept them for who they were. For example, when MLB introduced Billy Bean in his new ambassadorship role at the 2014 All-Star Break, the league recognized Glenn Burke, a gay baseball player of the 1970s. The league invited Burke's family to the ceremony. In a *New York Times* interview before the game, Burke's sister, Lutha Burke, said,

MLB Ambassador for Inclusion Billy Bean speaks at a PFLAG gala in 2015 to support the work that organization does for LGBTQ+ communities. In 2016 MLB promoted Bean to Vice President for Social Responsibility and Inclusion. Curtis Pride took over for Bean as MLB Ambassador for Inclusion. Pride, who is deaf, is also a baseball coach at Gallaudet University, a school in Washington, DC, for deaf and hard-of-hearing students.

*People are missing out when they decide to let a segment of our
society not be what they can truly be. . . . Maybe [my brother]
didn't get a chance to live out his dream. . . . He used to sleep in his
baseball uniform, and Mom used to have to peel it off him. But
make sure that other little boys get a chance to live out their dream.
Glenn would be very proud [to see his life made a difference].
Something good has come out of [his struggle] in the end.*

## MORE CHAPTERS IN MICHAEL SAM'S STORY

After Michael Sam came out in 2014, Dave Kopay wrote Sam an open
letter of encouragement on *Outsports*. Kopay wrote,

*Not only am I excited for you, I am excited for the NFL. I know
the [Southeastern Conference, Sam's college football conference]
is thanking its lucky stars that a player like you has succeeded
and developed, and it would be a significant thing for the
entire sports world and for you to continue on your path in
the National Football League. But know that now that you
are "publicly out" as a gay man you must focus on doing your
job and don't let any naysayers bring you down. You are no
wallflower and you can handle whatever crap comes your way.
You will bring it like you never have before.*

Yet Sam's career hasn't quite evolved the way Kopay assumed
it would. When Sam signed his deal with the Montreal Alouettes,
an interviewer asked the team's general manager, Jim Popp, if the
Alouettes had considered Sam's sexuality when the team made its
decision to sign him. Popp was clear in his reply: "Yes, he's the first
openly gay CFL player. But he's no different than any player we've
ever recruit[ed]. We recruited him strictly off his skill set, which is
that he's an outstanding pass-rusher." However, after sitting out the

first five games of the season and not making a single tackle in the one game he played, Sam left the Alouettes in August 2015, citing mental health reasons. *Outsports* editor Cyd Zeigler said, "When you decide to be a trailblazer, sometimes that trail gets awfully bumpy."

It's hard to know if football has seen the last of Michael Sam or what his impact on the sport will be for other LGBTQ+ players. Maybe another pro football player will come out—and while still actively playing in the NFL. Maybe that person will be able to withstand the intense scrutiny that will be part of coming out. Sam has said this about the future of gay players in the NFL: "Some thought others would join me [in coming out]. I did, too. . . . But it never happened. . . . It will."

## WHERE TO GO FROM HERE

The ninety-five hundred participants in the 2014 *Out on the Fields* survey ranked a series of solutions to combating homophobia in sports. The top three solutions were these:

- TAKE HOMOPHOBIA AND BULLYING SERIOUSLY—MAKE SURE PLAYERS, COACHES, SCHOOLS, AND PARENTS ARE AWARE OF HOMOPHOBIA AND BULLYING ON SPORTS TEAMS.

- MAKE SURE NATIONAL SPORTS ORGANIZATIONS ADOPT AND PROMOTE CLEAR ANTI-HOMOPHOBIA AND LGB INCLUSION POLICIES, BOTH AT THE PROFESSIONAL AND AMATEUR LEVEL.

- ENCOURAGE LGB SPORTS STARS TO COME OUT OF THE CLOSET, TO SET AN EXAMPLE.

Participants also suggested additional strategies, including these:

- USE THE MEDIA TO EDUCATE THE PUBLIC.

- WORK TO CHANGE SOCIETY SO THERE'S MORE ACCEPTANCE FOR LGB INDIVIDUALS.

- MAKE SURE PARENTS, COACHES, AND TEACHERS ARE MODELING ACCEPTANCE FOR ALL PLAYERS, ESPECIALLY LGBT PLAYERS.

- PROVIDE ONGOING ADVOCACY AND SUPPORT FOR LGB PLAYERS FROM FAMOUS ATHLETES.

According to the report's authors, athletes who come out feel even more bonded to their team, even with the reality of homophobia in the sporting world. And the goal, as the authors say, is to make coming out a nonissue:

*It would seem that the brave athletes who come out of the closet in sport help others to do the same and in turn, this increased visibility seems to lead to reductions in homophobic behaviour. However, it shouldn't require bravery to "come out." Parents, coaches, teachers and sporting organisations have a responsibility to make "coming out" a non-event by ensuring LGB athletes who decide to come out of the closet are supported and protected. Spectators also need to be willing to accept the reality that many of their sporting heroes, particularly in male sport, might be gay.*

All the athletes in this book—and countless more to come—with their courage and strength, can be heroes for young LGBTQ+ players who will come out in the future. Culture at large will continue to change, toward inclusivity, as will the culture of sports. LGBTQ+ athletes, coaches, and others in the sporting world are coming out in greater numbers every year, leading the way in creating safe, supportive environments where LGBTQ+ athletes can, will, and must continue to claim themselves and their fields.

# AN OPEN LETTER FROM A GAY COLLEGE FOOTBALL PLAYER

*Eric Lueshen was a kicker with the University of Nebraska Huskers from 2003 through 2006. He answered a teammate's query of "Are you gay?" with a "Yes" in fall 2003 and was out with his coaches and other players from then on. Though Lueshen is confident the media knew of his sexual identity, no story about him ever appeared in local or national press coverage. Lueshen isn't sure if the University of Nebraska wanted to keep it quiet or whether the media felt that both the conservative state of Nebraska and the country weren't ready for a gay college football player. His announcement to his teammates came more than ten years before Michael Sam's. Lueshen shares his thoughts in this open letter to young athletes.*

Dear Closeted Athlete,

I've always said that the first steps toward true happiness are fully accepting yourself and being true to yourself. In the end, you have to live your life the best and most honest way you possibly can. Being anything other than your authentic self doesn't benefit you; it ultimately deters you from happiness and many of the wonderful gifts life has to offer.

For many years, I struggled with accepting the fact that I am a gay man. I hid in the closet, afraid of what others may think. Would my parents kick me out? Would I be made fun of more than I already was at school? Would my teammates accept me? Would my coaches kick me off their teams or bench me? All in all, I was driving myself into a deep and dark hole of stress, depression, and misery.

In time, I realized that one's sexuality is only a small characteristic and nothing that defines them. People should be judged for their morals, character, and values. If someone wants to judge another person for their sexuality, that is their choice. I've always said that if someone chooses to make my sexuality an issue, then that's THEIR problem . . . NOT mine. One's sexuality is something to be celebrated, not hidden. The day I made the decision to no longer let other people control my own happiness and to come out was the first moment I truly felt alive; no longer clouded by the polluted thinking of worry and fear.

You too have the opportunity to take control of your own happiness. Once you've made that first step, you're faced with finding the courage to tell your family, friends, teammates, and coaches. I guarantee that you have the strength and courage within yourself to take this next step. And remember, no matter how much you may feel otherwise, you are not alone. There are a lot of successful LGBTQ+ athletes living openly in this world, and each day more athletes are coming out. These athletes, along with the rest of the LGBTQ+ community, are always here to support you. We are a family.

Was it easy for me to come out to my fellow Husker football teammates? No. Was it worth it? Absolutely. I never could have imagined how much support I'd receive, how many peoples' minds would be opened, and how many lives I'd change (including my own) just by being true to myself and no longer living a lie. Even the people whose potential reactions I had feared the most eventually surprised me [by being accepting]. As you start to come out to your teammates and coaches, I'm certain you will experience similar surprises as well.

The times have changed a lot since I played college football. America and the sports world are ready to embrace LGBTQ+ athletes. These athletes are now being measured by their abilities, character, and leadership, not by their sexual orientation or gender identity. People realize that if you can play, you can play.

I wish you all the best in your endeavor to live life as your authentic self. Know that you are brave enough, you are strong enough, and that you are not alone. This is your life, no one else's. I encourage each of you to take control of your own happiness. Always remember that life begins on the other side of fear.

Sincerely,
Eric Lueshen

# TIMELINE

*To keep up with the ever-changing world of LGBTQ+ sports, check Outsports.com on a regular basis. Many of these timeline events can be found there, and the site is regularly updated with new LGBTQ+ milestones.*

**1932:** Babe Didrikson Zaharias wins a gold medal for track and field in the Olympic Games. Best known for golfing, she also competes in tennis, baseball, softball, and basketball. Her female partner, Betty Dodd, is at her bedside when she dies in 1956. She never publicly comes out as a lesbian.

**1948:** Tennis great Bill Tilden (William Tatem Tilden II) comes out as a gay man in his autobiography.

**1968:** The International Olympic Committee institutes mandatory sex testing for all female athletes.

**1972:** Title IX passes, stating no one in the United States can be excluded from participation in, or discriminated against while participating in, any educational program or activity receiving federal funding based on their sex. Title IX is used in the early twenty-first century to protect transgender, gender diverse, and lesbian and gay individuals in K–12 schools.

**1975:** Retired NFL running back Dave Kopay comes out as the first gay football player in a *Washington Post* series about homosexual athletes.

**1976:** British figure skater John Curry comes out in February 1976 and becomes the first openly gay Olympic gold medalist.

Transgender women's tennis player Renée Richards is barred by the United States Tennis Association from competing as a woman in the 1976 US Open. She takes the USTA to court and wins the discrimination lawsuit in 1977.

**1981:** Women's tennis player Billie Jean King is outed when former partner Marilyn Barnett files a "galimony" suit.

Tennis player Martina Navratilova comes out in an article in the *New York Daily News*.

**1982:** Olympic track-and-field runner Tom Waddell founds the Gay Olympics (later the Gay Games), which hosted its first games in San Francisco.

**1986:** Retired Washington Redskins tight end Jerry Smith dies of AIDS.

**1989:** Bodybuilder and Mr. America and Mr. Universe titleholder Bob Paris comes out as gay.

**1993:** Boxer Savoy Howe becomes the first openly lesbian boxer.

**1994:** Diver and Olympic gold medalist Greg Louganis comes out as a gay man at the Gay Games in New York City.

**1995:** Retired LA Dodgers and Oakland A's outfielder Glenn Burke dies from complications from AIDS.

**1996:** With the support of Martina Navratilova, the Women's Sports Foundation launches the Project to Eliminate Homophobia in Sport. It is later renamed It Takes a Team! Education Campaign for LGBT Issues in Sport.

**1997:** Dan Woog's book *Jocks* is published, detailing the lives of dozens of openly gay athletes.

**1998:** The book *Strong Women, Deep Closets: Lesbians and Homophobia in Sport* by Pat Griffin is published. It is the first book to detail homophobic discrimination in women's sports.

Mike Muska becomes the new athletic director of Oberlin College, making him the first openly gay man to hold such a position.

ESPN airs the television special *World of the Gay Athlete.*

**1999:** The International Olympic Committee ends mandatory sex testing for women athletes.

Cyd Zeigler and Jim Buzinski create *Outsports*, a resource for gay sports fans and athletes.

**2001:** Sportswriter Bill Konigsberg comes out as gay on the front page of *ESPN.com.*

The National Center for Lesbian Rights initiates the Sports Project, focusing on legal and advocacy support for coaches and athletes facing discrimination due to gender identity or sexual orientation.

**2002:** Starting softball catcher Andrea Zimbardi settles a lawsuit against the University of Florida after being dismissed from the team because of her sexual orientation.

WNBA athlete Sue Wicks comes out as a lesbian.

Team cocaptain and defensive tackle Brian Sims comes out as gay while playing Division II football for Bloomsburg University in Pennsylvania.

Retired NFL defensive tackle Esera Tuaolo comes out as gay on HBO's *Real Sports.*

**2003:** The University of Pennsylvania founds Penn Athletes and Allies Tackling Homophobia (PATH), a student-athlete group that seeks to eliminate homophobia in sports. It is the first group of its kind.

The Gay and Lesbian Athletics Foundation in Cambridge, Massachusetts, holds the first National Gay & Lesbian Athletics Conference, which becomes an annual event.

The National Collegiate Athletic Association begins offering training about sexual orientation issues in sports, available for free to all member schools.

**2004:** The International Olympic Committee adopts the Stockholm consensus outlining the rules and regulations for transsexual athletic participation in the Olympic Games.

**2005:** USA Track and Field adopts a transsexual participation policy similar to the Stockholm consensus.

The United States Golf Association institutes a policy similar to the IOC's Stockholm consensus regulating participation of transsexual athletes.

Track-and-field athlete Keelin Godsey comes out as transgender, making him the first openly transgender athlete competing in the NCAA.

Three-time Women's National Basketball Association MVP and Olympic champion basketball player Sheryl Swoopes comes out as a lesbian in an *ESPN the Magazine* article.

**2006:** Openly lesbian tennis professional Amélie Mauresmo wins Wimbledon.

**2007:** Retired NBA athlete John Amaechi became the first professional basketball player to come out as gay.

In April the Washington Interscholastic Activities Association passes the first policy allowing the participation of transgender athletes in their identified gender in high school sport.

GLAAD hires Ted Rybka as the first director of sports media. His role is to monitor how the media covers LGBTQ+ issues in sports.

**2008:** Eleven openly gay, lesbian, and bisexual athletes compete in the Beijing Olympics, winning seven medals. Australian diver Matthew Mitcham, the only openly gay man competing, wins a gold medal.

German pole vaulter Balian Buschbaum comes out as a transgender man.

**2009:** Portland State University women's basketball coach Sherri Murrell becomes the first NCAA Division I coach to be an out lesbian.

Miami (Ohio) University hockey team student manager Brendan Burke comes out. He is killed in an automobile accident in February 2010.

Openly lesbian women's basketball coach Lorri Sulpizio wins a lawsuit against Mesa Community College in Arizona for having been fired without just cause.

**2010:** The It Gets Better Project, to help prevent suicide among LGBTQ+ youth, posts its first video.

Basketball player Kye Allums becomes the first openly transgender NCAA Division I college athlete.

**2011:** The Gay, Lesbian, & Straight Education Network (GLSEN) launches Changing the Game: The GLSEN Sports Project. The project is dedicated to making K–12 sports a safe and welcoming environment for students of all sexual orientations and gender expressions/identities.

The NBA fines Kobe Bryant $100,000 for using a homophobic slur toward an official.

Rick Welts, the president of the Phoenix Suns, comes out as gay.

The NCAA adopts an inclusion policy for transgender athletes.

Major League Soccer player David Testo comes out as a gay man. He is the first MLS player to do so.

The National Football League, the National Hockey League, Major League Baseball, and the National Basketball Association adopt nondiscrimination policies that include sexual orientation.

**2012:** NHL scout Patrick Burke launches the You Can Play Project.

US soccer player and Olympic and World Cup champion Megan Rapinoe comes out as a lesbian.

Nike hosts the first LGBT Sports Summit.

Partnered with *Compete Magazine*, a publication about LGBTQ+ athletes, Campus Pride releases a "Top 10" list of LGBTQ-friendly colleges.

Boxer Orlando Cruz comes out as gay.

**2013:** Olympic women's hockey medalist Caitlin Cahow comes out as a lesbian.

NBA player Jason Collins comes out as a gay man on the front cover of *Sports Illustrated*.

**2014:** University of Missouri defensive end Michael Sam comes out. He is the first openly gay player to be drafted into the NFL.

Derrick Gordon, basketball player for the University of Massachusetts–Amherst, comes out as gay. He is the first openly gay man to play college basketball.

Defending NCAA champion shot-putter Tina Hillman, from Iowa State University, comes out as pansexual (sexual or romantic attraction to a person regardless of sex or gender identity).

World-champion Australian swimmer Ian Thorpe comes out as a gay man.

**2015:** The ruling in the US Supreme Court case *Obergefell v. Hodges* makes same-sex marriage legal in all fifty states.

Caitlyn Jenner comes out as transgender.

David Denson, a minor-league player in the Milwaukee Brewers farm system, comes out as a gay man.

Professional wrestler "Money" Matt Cage comes out as a gay man.

Through the publication of a personal essay on *Outsports* in October, Chris Burns becomes the first openly gay Division I men's basketball coach.

Women's basketball coach Curt Miller is hired by the Connecticut Suns, making him the first openly gay man to coach a professional sports team in North America.

Los Angeles Dodgers executive Eric Braverman comes out as gay.

**2016:** Former outfielder Curtis Pride is named MLB's Ambassador for Inclusion.

# SOURCE NOTES

10  Emanuella Grinberg, "David Denson Makes History as First Openly Gay Active Player in Baseball," *CNN*, August 16, 2015, http://www.cnn.com /2015/08/16/us/david-denson-baseball-gay-feat/.

11  Mary Wisniewski and Ben Klayman, "Milwaukee Brewers Minor-League Player Comes Out as Gay: Report," *Reuters*, August 16, 2015, http://www.reuters.com/article/2015/08/16/us-usa-baseball-gay -idUSKCN0QL0KE20150816.

12  Erik Denison and Alistair Kitchen, *Out on the Field: The First International Study on Homophobia in Sport* (Rosebury, NSW, Australia: Repucom, 2015), 39.

12  Ibid., 46.

17  Pat Griffin, ed., *Strong Women, Deep Closets: Lesbians and Homophobia in Sport* (Champaign, IL: Human Kinetics, 1998), 16.

17–18  Ibid., 25.

18  Ibid., 17.

19  Allie Grasgreen, "Gag Orders on Sexuality," *Inside Higher Ed*, May 23, 2013, https://www.insidehighered.com/news/2013/05/23/baylors-gag-order -athletes-sexuality-reveals-homophobia-still-prevalent-womens.

20  Rachel Blount, "3 Former Duluth Coaches File Discrimination Lawsuit," *Minneapolis Star Tribune*, September 28, 2015, http://www.startribune.com /3-former-duluth-coaches-file-discrimination-lawsuit/329788221/.

21  Pat Griffin, "College Sports' War on Female Coaches," *Outsports*, January 29, 2015, http://www.outsports.com/2015/1/29/7923853/women-coach-college -sports-pat-griffin.

21  Matt Vensel, "Vikings Coach Priefer Suspended 3 Games After Kluwe Investigation," *Minneapolis Star Tribune*, July 19, 2014, http://www .startribune.com/local/267734931.html?page=1&c=y.

22  David Fleming, "Nothing to See Here: A History of Showers in Sports," *ESPN the Magazine*, July 8, 2014, http://espn.go.com/espn/feature/story/_/id /11169006/nfl-showers-hostile-environment-michael-sam-espn-magazine.

22  Ibid.

23  Matthew Tharrett, "Charles Barkley: The Whole 'Locker Room Discussion' Is 'an Insult to Gay People,'" *Queerty*, February 18, 2014, http://www.queerty .com/charles-barkley-the-whole-locker-room-discussion-is-an-insult-to-gay -people-20140218.

24  Kiley Kroh, "In the Goal, and Out of the Closet, at the Women's World Cup," *Think Progress*, June 30, 2015, http://thinkprogress.org/sports/2015/06/30 /3675611/goal-closet-womens-world-cup/.

24  Grant Wahl, "U.S. Finds Inspiration in Supreme Court Ruling for WWC Win over China," *Sports Illustrated*, June 27, 2015, http://www.si.com/planet -futbol/2015/06/26/uswnt-china-supreme-court-marriage-equality -wambach-womens-world-cup.

25  Jerry Portwood, "Fever Pitch," *Out*, July 2, 2012, http://www.out.com/travel -nightlife/london/2012/07/02/fever-pitch.

27  Alissa Greenberg, "Abby Wambach Kissing Her Wife after Winning the World Cup Will Warm Your Heart, *Time*, July 6, 2015, http://time.com /3946226/abby-wambach-womens-soccer-world-cup-wife-kiss-lgbt-gay -marriage/.

30  Eric Marcus, "Dave Kopay," in *Making History: The Struggle for Gay and Lesbian Equal Rights, 1945-1990, an Oral History* (New York: HarperCollins, 1992), 276.

30  Ibid.

31  Ibid.

31  Ibid.

33  Amy Goodman, "Tennis Star Martina Navratilova, among First 'Out' Pro Athletes, Congratulates NBA's Jason Collins," *Democracy Now!*, May 1, 2013, http://www.democracynow.org/2013/5/1/tennis_star_martina_ navratilova_among_first.

33  Jim Buzinski, "Moment #3: Tennis Great Billie Jean King Outed," *Outsports*, October 2, 2011, http://www.outsports.com/2011/10/2/4051938/moment-3 -tennis-great-billie-jean-king-outed.

34  Associated Press, "Billie Jean King Talks Coming Out," *ESPN*, August 6, 2013, http://espn.go.com/tennis/story/_/id/9545526/billie-jean-king -discusses-coming-pbs-show.

35  Jason Collins, "Why NBA Center Jason Collins Is Coming Out Now," *Sports Illustrated*, last modified June 20, 2014, http://www.si.com/more-sports /2013/04/29/jason-collins-gay-nba-player.

35  Andrew Keh, "Jason Collins, First Openly Gay N.B.A. Player, Signs with Nets and Appears in Game," *New York Times*, February 23, 2014, http:// www.nytimes.com/2014/02/24/sports/basketball/after-signing-with-nets -jason-collins-becomes-first-openly-gay-nba-player.html?_r=0.

36  Philip Galanes, "Speak Your Own Truth, on Your Own Terms: Billie Jean King and Jason Collins on Being Gay Athletes," *New York Times*, June 27, 2014, http://www.nytimes.com/2014/06/29/fashion/billie-jean-king-and -jason-collins-on-being-gay-athletes.html.

37   George Solomon, "Ex-Redskin Jerry Smith Says He's Battling AIDS: 'Maybe It Will Help People Understand,'" *Washington Post*, August 26, 1986, https://www.washingtonpost.com/sports/redskins/ex-redskin-jerry-smith-says-hes-battlingaidsmaybe-it-will-help-people-understand/2011/12/01/gIQAJAA4GO_story.html.

38   "Glenn Burke, 42, a Major League Baseball Player," *New York Times*, June 2, 1995, http://www.nytimes.com/1995/06/02/nyregion/glenn-burke-42-a-major-league-baseball-player.html.

38   Sarah Kaplan, "The Trials of Baseball's First Openly Gay Player, Glenn Burke, Four Decades Ago," *Washington Post*, August 17, 2015, http://www.washingtonpost.com/news/morning-mix/wp/2015/08/17/the-trials-of-baseballs-first-openly-gay-player-glenn-burke-four-decades-ago/.

39   Cyd Zeigler, "Moment #95: Muffin Spencer-Devlin Becomes First Pro Golfer to Come Out," *Outsports*, July 10, 2011, http://www.outsports.com/2011/7/10/4051498/moment-95-muffin-spencer-devlin-becomes-first-pro-golfer-to-come-out.

40   "WWE Releases Statement in Support of Darren Young," *WWE*, August 15, 2013, http://www.wwe.com/inside/wwe-releases-statement-on-darren-young-26140515.

42   Kate Fagan, "UMass's Derrick Gordon Says He's Gay," *ESPN*, April 9, 2014, http://espn.go.com/mens-college-basketball/story/_/id/10754694/derrick-gordon-umass-basketball-player-becomes-first-openly-gay-ncaa-division-player.

43   Tyler Lockman, "Gay ASU Lineman Comes Out with a Message: Be Who You Are," *Fox Sports Arizona,* August 14, 2014, www.foxsports.com/arizona/story/gay-asu-lineman-comes-out-with-a-message-be-who-you-are-081414.

43   Ibid.

44   Cyd Ziegler, "South Carolina College with Two Gay Athletes Bans Homosexuality in the Name of God," *Outsports*, February 26, 2015, http://www.outsports.com/2015/2/26/8112495/erskine-college-gay-athletes-ban.

44   "#ProudToPlay: Celebrating Equality for All Athletes," *YouTube*, June 3, 2014, http://youtube-global.blogspot.com/2014/06/proudtoplay.html.

45   Derek Schell, "After Coming Out College Basketball Player Finds Passion for Sport at All-Time High," *Outsports*, October 7, 2013, http://www.outsports.com/2013/10/7/4810058/derek-schell-hillsdale-college-basketball-ncaa-gay-coming-out-story.

47   Donna Rose, "Transsexual Athletes Treated Unfairly," *CNN*, October 20, 2010, http://www.cnn.com/2010/OPINION/10/18/rose.transsexuals.sports/index.html.

49    Alex Jackson Nelson, e-mail correspondence with the author, December 2, 2015.

51-52  John Branch, "Dutee Chand, Female Sprinter with High Testosterone Level, Wins Right to Compete," *New York Times*, July 27, 2015, http://www.nytimes .com/2015/07/28/sports/international/dutee-chand-female-sprinter-with -high-male-hormone-level-wins-right-to-compete.html?_r=0.

52    Ibid.

52    Rebecca Jordan-Young and Katrina Karkazis, "You Say You're a Woman? That Should Be Enough," *New York Times*, June 17, 2012, http://www .nytimes.com/2012/06/18/sports/olympics/olympic-sex-verification-you-say -youre-a-woman-that-should-be-enough.html?_r=0.

54-55  "Transgender Woman Barred from U.S. Open 39 Years Ago Today," *AOL*, August 27, 2015, http://www.aol.com/article/2015/08/27/transgender -barred-from-us-open-39-years-ago-today/21228019/.

55    Michael Hainey, "The Woman Who Paved the Way for Men to Become Women," *GQ*, May 26, 2015, http://www.gq.com/story/renee-richards -interview.

55    Jos Truitt, "Fallon Fox on Life as a Trans Athlete: 'The Scope of Vitriol and Anger was Mind-Blowing,'" *Guardian* (US), February 16, 2015, http://www .theguardian.com/sport/2015/feb/16/fallon-fox-trans-mma-athlete -interview.

57    Amelia Gapin, "I Am a Transgender Woman with Mental Illness and I Am a Finalist to Be on the Cover of Women's Running," *entirely amelia* (blog), October 3, 2015, http://www.entirelyamelia.com/2015/10/03/im-a-finalist -to-be-on-the-cover-of-womens-running/.

57    Ibid.

58    Parker Marie Molloy, "Heroes, Martyrs, and Myths: The Battle for the Rights of Transgender Athletes," *Vice*, November 6, 2014, https://sports .vice.com/article/heroes-martyrs-and-myths-the-battle-for-the-rights-of -transgender-athletes.

59    Katy Steinmetz, "Meet the First Openly Transgender NCAA Division I Athlete," *Time*, October 28, 2014, http://time.com/3537849/meet-the -first-openly-transgender-ncaa-athlete/.

60    Kye Allums, "How I've Turned My Struggle as the NCAA's First Transgender Athlete into Acceptance," *Playboy*, October 9, 2013, http://playboysfw.kinja .com/i-was-the-ncaas-first-transgender-basketball-player-an-1442780215.

60    Buzz Bissinger, "He Says Goodbye, She Says Hello," *Vanity Fair*, July 2015, 62.

62    Sally Tamarkin, "8 Transgender Athletes Explain How Fitness and Movement Changed Their Lives," *BuzzFeed*, February 6, 2015, http://www .buzzfeed.com/sallytamarkin/transgender-athletes.

62 Ibid.

63 *Daily* news staff, "Transcript: Caitlyn Jenner's ESPYs Acceptance Speech for Arthur Ashe Courage Award," *New York Daily News*, July 16, 2015, http://www.nydailynews.com/entertainment/tv/transcript-caitlyn-jenner-espys -acceptance-speech-article-1.2293939.

64 Nadia Khomami, "Ian Thorpe Comes Out as Gay in Parkinson Interview," *Guardian* (US), July 13, 2014, http://www.theguardian.com/sport/2014 /jul/12/ian-thorpe-gay-parkinson-interview.

65 "NHL Becomes First North American Sports League to Have All Teams Support LGBT Athletes and Fans," *Huffington Post*, January 23, 2014, http://www.huffingtonpost.com/2014/01/08/nhl-lgbt-support-all -teams_n_4562379.html.

66 "Mission Statement," You Can Play, accessed October 24, 2015, http:// youcanplay.org/pages/mission-statement.

67 Patrick Burke, "Never Forgotten: Patrick Burke Remembers His Pioneering Brother, Brendan," *Outsports*, June 20, 2010, http://www.outsports.com /2010/6/20/3863336/never-forgotten-patrick-burke-remembers-his -pioneering-brother-brendan.

69 "NCAA LGBTQ Subcommittee Statement of Affirmation," NCAA, accessed March 10, 2015, http://www.ncaa.org/about/resources/inclusion/LGBTQ -resources.

70 National Center for Lesbian Rights, "Groundbreaking Nike LGBT Sports Summit Takes on Bullying, Homophobia, and Transphobia in Sports," news release, June 18, 2012, http://www.nclrights.org/press-room/press-release /groundbreaking-nike-lgbt-sports-summit-takes-on-bullying-homophobia -and-transphobia-in-sports/.

71 "MN State High School League Transgender Policy," Child Protection League Action!, accessed February 14, 2015, http://cplaction.com/hs -athletics/.

72 Child M's mother, e-mail interview with the author, October 23, 2015.

73–74 Elliott Kunerth, e-mail interview with the author, March 7, 2015.

74 "How To File a Discrimination Complaint with the Office of Civil Rights," US Department of Education, accessed October 16, 2015, http://www2 .ed.gov/about/offices/list/ocr/docs/howto.html.

75 Ibid.

77 Chloie Jönsson, "I Transformed My Body in the Ultimate Way," *Self*, July 15, 2015, http://www.self.com/wellness/2015/07/transformed-my-body -ultimate-way/.

79    Derek Helling, "Transgender High School Cheerleader Happy to Be One of the Girls," *Outsports*, September 9, 2015, http://www.outsports.com/2015/9/9/9283443/transgender-high-school-cheerleader-landon-patterson.

80    "Five-Time Freeski Champ, Sochi Silver Medalist Gus Kenworthy Comes Out as Gay," *ESPN*, October 22, 2015, http://espn.go.com/olympics/story/_/id/13942305/olympic-freeskier-x-games-star-gus-kenworthy-first-openly-gay-action-sports-athlete.

81    John Branch, "Posthumous Recognition: M.L.B. to Recognize Glenn Burke as Baseball's Gay Pioneer," *New York Times*, July 14, 2014, http://www.nytimes.com/2014/07/15/sports/baseball/mlb-to-recognize-glenn-burke-as-a-gay-pioneer-in-baseball.html?_r=1.

81    David Kopay, "Read David Kopay's Open Letter to Michael Sam," *Outsports*, February 11, 2014, http://www.outsports.com/2014/2/11/5397016/dave-kopay-michael-sam-gay-nfl.

81    Dan Hanzus, "Michael Sam Signs Deal with CFL's Montreal Alouettes," *NFL*, May 22, 2015, http://www.nfl.com/news/story/0ap3000000493902/article/michael-sam-signs-deal-with-cfls-montreal-alouettes.

82    Trudy Ring, "Michael Sam Leaves Pro Football, Cites Mental Health Concerns," *Advocate*, August 15, 2015, http://www.advocate.com/sports/2015/08/15/michael-sam-leaving-pro-football-cites-mental-health-concerns.

82    Andrew Corsello, "Michael the Brave," *GQ*, November 12, 2014, http://www.gq.com/moty/2014/michael-sam-men-of-the-year-game-changer.

83    Denison and Kitchen, *Out on the Field*, 70.

84–85  Eric Lueshen, e-mail message to author, February 18, 2015.

# GLOSSARY

**bisexual:** a person who is attracted to individuals of both sexes, though not necessarily to equal degrees. The attraction may be romantic, sexual, or both.

**cisgender:** an individual whose gender identity matches the sex assigned at birth. The Latin prefix *cis* means "on the same side."

**feminine:** to possess or express characteristics, traits, or both that are traditionally assigned to females

**gay:** a male or masculine-identified person who is attracted to other male-identified individuals, romantically, sexually, or both. This term applies to both men or women who feel same-sex attraction.

**gender binary:** a model of gender identity that classifies gender in two separate, distinct realms—male and female

**gender confirmation surgery:** a surgical procedure or set of procedures that changes a person's anatomical body to conform to that person's gender identity

**gender dysphoria:** the medical term (and the term used by insurance companies) for the condition in which a person's gender identity does not match the assigned sex at birth. The term also refers to the discomfort and distress a person feels in relation to the feeling of mismatch between assigned sex at birth and gender identity.

**gender fluid:** a gender identity that may shift and change. A gender fluid person may identify as male, female, neutral, or any other gender identity.

**gender identity:** a person's inner sense of being male, female, both, or neither

**gender presentation/gender expression:** a range of characteristics that may signal an individual's gender identity. Gender expression and gender presentation can include clothes, behaviors, vocal characteristics, jobs, and activities.

**genderqueer:** a person who does not subscribe to traditional binary gender behaviors or appearances. That person may have a gender identity of neither male nor female or both or somewhere in between male and female.

**homophobia:** a range of feelings of fear, mistrust, or dislike of people who are homosexual, or discrimination against individuals who are homosexual

**hormone replacement therapy:** medically prescribed administration of estrogen or testosterone to help transgender individuals align their gender identities and their bodies. For example, the male hormone testosterone will deepen the voice, increase muscle mass, and promote hair growth while the female hormone estrogen will make the voice higher, promote breast growth, and provide redistribution of body fat.

**hyperandrogenism:** also known as androgen (male hormone) excess, this is a condition of high levels of androgens and the associated effects of those high androgens

**intersex:** a physical condition in which a person has some combination of both female and male internal or external or both sexual organs. An individual who is intersex may also have various combinations of chromosomes instead of the traditional XX (female) or XY (male) pattern.

**lesbian:** a female or feminine-identified person who is attracted to other female-identified individuals, romantically, sexually, or both

**masculine:** to possess characteristics or traits that are traditionally assigned to males

**misogyny:** the belief (personal, cultural, or both) that perpetuates a hatred of women or feminine characteristics. This belief leads to mistreatment and less-than-equal treatment of women in society.

**pansexual:** sexual or romantic attraction to a person regardless of sex or gender identity

**queer:** the word usually indicates an open, nonbinary or both sexuality (outside the binary of gay and straight). It can also refer to an open or fluid gender presentation or to an open, liberal, and inclusive political stance toward LGBTQ+ issues.

**sex chromosomes:** the genetic markers in a human body that determine the features of human biological sex. Usually the sex chromosomes of a female body are XX, and the sex chromosomes of a male body are XY.

**sexual orientation:** a term that expresses the gender configuration of a person's romantic, sexual partnerships, whether that be same-gender attraction, opposite gender attraction, or something else. Commonly recognized sexual orientations are lesbian, gay, straight, and bisexual, but there are others, such as pansexuality or asexuality (no romantic or sexual attraction to anyone).

**transgender:** people whose gender identity is different from the gender identity associated with their assigned sex at birth. Trans people may or may not choose to undergo medical intervention or to pursue legal or informal procedures to align gender and biological identities.

**transition:** the period of time during which a person begins living as their actual gender. Transitioning may include hormone therapy, gender confirmation surgery, a name change, or changes to legal documents to reflect one's true gender.

**trans man:** a transsexual person who was assigned a female identity at birth but identifies as a male. A trans man has usually had some form of medical intervention to align his gender and biological identities.

**transphobia:** a range of feelings of fear, mistrust, or dislike of people who are transgender, or discrimination against people who are transgender

**trans woman:** a transsexual person who was assigned a male identity at birth but now identifies as a female. A trans woman has usually had some form of medical intervention to align her gender and biological identities.

# SELECTED BIBLIOGRAPHY

Aitchison, Cara Carmichael, ed. *Sport and Gender Identities: Masculinities, Femininities, and Sexualities*. London: Routledge, 2007.

Bean, Billy. *Going the Other Way: An Intimate Memoir of Life In and Out of Major League Baseball*. With Chris Bull. Reissue ed. New York: The Experiment, 2014.

Denison, Erik, and Alistair Kitchen. *Out on the Fields: The First International Study on Homophobia in Sport*. Rosebury, NSW, Australia: Repucom, 2015.

"The Good Fight," in "Rites of Passage," *Snap Judgment,* no. 602. First broadcast January 23, 2015, by National Public Radio. Hosted by Glynn Washingotn. Distributed by the WNYC.

Griffin, Pat. *Strong Women, Deep Closets: Lesbians and Homophobia in Sport*. Champaign, IL: Human Kinetics, 1998.

Kamal, Rana. "Transgender Student Athletes." *Our Issues Twin Cities*, The CW23 (WUCW), YouTube video, 22:05, January 2, 2015. https://www.youtube.com/watch?v=3RIC9slWaH4.

Kopay, David. "The Jock." In *Making History: The Struggle for Gay and Lesbian Equal Rights 1945-1990, an Oral History*. Edited by Eric Marcus. New York: HarperCollins, 1992.

Lunt, David J. "The Heroic Athlete in Ancient Greece." *Journal of Sport History* 36, no. 3 (Fall 2009): 375–392.

Warren, Patricia Nell. *The Lavender Locker Room: 3,000 Years of Great Athletes Whose Sexual Orientation Was Different*. Glendale, CA: Wildcat, 2006.

# FURTHER INFORMATION

## Books

Amaechi, John. *Man in the Middle*. New York: ESPN Books, 2007.

Burke, Glenn, and Erik Sherman. *Out at Home: The True Story of Glenn Burke, Baseball's First Openly Gay Player*. New York: Berkley, 2015.

Louganis, Greg. *Breaking the Surface*. With Eric Marcus. 2nd ed. Naperville, IL: Sourcebooks, 2006.

Richards, Renée. *No Way Renée: The Second Half of My Notorious Life*. New York: Simon and Schuster, 2007.

Rogers, Robbie. *Coming Out to Play*. New York: Penguin, 2014.

Tewksbury, Mark. *Inside Out: Straight Talk from a Gay Jock*. New York: HarperCollins, 2014.

Thomas, Gareth. *Proud: My Autobiography*. London: Ebury, 2014.

## Documentaries

Drath, Eric. *Renée*. Bristol, CT: ESPN Films, 2011.
This film covers the life of professional tennis player Renée Richards and her battle to enter the 1977 US Open as a transgender woman.

Furjanic, Cheryl, Will Sweeney, Karen K. H. Sim, and Diana Holtzberg. *Back on Board: Greg Louganis*. New York: BOB Films, 2014.
This film chronicles the life of Greg Louganis, from his success as an Olympic athlete to his financial crises. The film also discusses his life with HIV.

Harris, Doug, and Sean Maddison. *OUT: The Glenn Burke Story*. First broadcast November 10, 2010, by Comcast SportsNet Bay Area.
This film examines the baseball career and early death of gay baseball player Glenn Burke.

*Outside the Box*. PBS Student Reporting Labs. Public Broadcasting System, 2016.
This series by young reporters around the nation explores teens who are challenging LGBTQ+ and gender stereotyping in various fields, including sports.

*Out to Win*. Directed by Malcolm Ingram. Toronto: Brothers Double, 2015.
This film is a relatively comprehensive look at gay sports figures, past and present.

Thomas, Michiel. *Game Face*. Los Angeles: Michiel Thomas, 2015.
This documentary features the stories of Fallon Fox and other LGBTQ+ athletes.

*Training Rules*. Directed by Dee Mosbacher. San Francisco: WomanVision, 2009.
This film examines how women's sports deal with homophobia and how some players' dreams have been dashed by homophobic practices.

## Podcasts

Mosier, Chris. "Transgender Identity and Issues Faced by Trans People in Sports (Episodes 25–28)." Interview, March 9, 2015. *OutCasting*. http://mfpg.org/index.php/outcasting/87-outcasting/outcasting-episodes/179-outcasting-0025-0028. These interviews with Chris Mosier, an out transgender triathlete, cover transgender identity and the issues trans persons face in sports.

## Site to Visit

The National Gay and Lesbian Sports Hall of Fame
Center on Halsted
3656 N. Halsted Street
Chicago, IL 60613
This Hall of Fame has hosted four classes of inductees (2013, 2014, 2015, and 2016), including athletes, corporations, and others who have helped LGBTQ+ athletes succeed. Athlete nominees can include anyone from youth to professional players.

## Websites

The Center for Sport and Social Justice
http://www20.csueastbay.edu/ceas/departments/kin/CSSJ/
This center, housed at California State University East Bay in Hayward, California, promotes well-rounded thought about sports and its role in culture. The center's goal is to study and understand sport as a cultural practice and how sports can change people and communities. The center can also be found on Facebook.

GO! Athletes
http://www.goathletes.org/
This website provides networking for current and former LGBTQ+ athletes at the high school and college level. Networking opportunities include sharing individual stories to increase visibility, starting a GO! Athletes chapter, joining a GO! Athletes committee, and bringing a GO! Athletes panel to your school

NCAA LGBTQ+ Resources
http://www.ncaa.org/about/resources/inclusion/LGBTQ-resources
This website lists the NCAA's Best Practices for supporting and including LGBTQ+ athletes, along with other resources for creating support and inclusion in collegiate sports organizations.

*Outsports*
http://www.outsports.com/
This site features news stories about all kinds of LGBTQ+ athletes in every sport.

*Transas City*

http://transascity.org/cross-training-the-history-and-future-of-transgender-and-intersex-athletes-1/

This blog has an in-depth, well-researched series of posts about transgender athletes called "Cross-Training: The History and Future of Transgender and Intersex Athletes."

Trans*Athlete

http://www.transathlete.com/

Started by transgender triathlete Chris Mosier, the website is a strong resource for trans-inclusion ideas and features different resources for building trans-inclusive sports spaces. Especially helpful is the page on trans terminology as well as the page about trans-inclusive policies by sports organization (including the International Quidditch Association).

You Can Play Project

http://youcanplayproject.org/

This organization promotes respect for all athletes, especially LGBTQ+ players. The project also educates and trains straight allies to ensure respectful and inclusive playing conditions.

# INDEX

# PHOTO ACKNOWLEDGMENTS

The images in this book are used with the permission of: © iStockphoto.com/manx_in_the_world (rainbow flag); © Todd Strand/Independent Picture Service, p. 4; AP Photo/Stephen Smith/Four Seam Images, p. 10; © Leon Bennett/Getty Images, p. 12; © Jason LaVeris/FilmMagic/Getty Images, p. 14; © Cooper Neill/Getty Images, p. 19; AP Photo/Richard Tsong-Taatarii/Star Tribune, p. 20; AP Photo/Evan Pinkus, p. 22; © Alex Menendez/Getty Images, p. 25; © Kevin C. Cox/Getty Images, p. 26; © Everett Collection Historical/Alamy, p. 29; AP Photo/Pro Football Hall of Fame, p. 30; © Keystone Pictures USA/Alamy, p. 32; © Daily Mail/Rex/Alamy, p. 34; © Megan Mack/Getty Images, p. 35; AP Photo/LM, p. 38; © Neal Preston/Corbis, p. 39; © Dave Spencer/Splash News/Corbis, p. 40; © D Dipasupil/WireImage for PFLAG National/Getty Images, p. 41; © Mitchell Layton/Getty Images, p. 43; AP Photo/Noah Berger p. 46; © Alexander Hassenstein/Getty Images for IAAF, p. 51; © Marvin Joseph/The Washington Post/Getty Images, p. 53; © Bettmann/Corbis, p. 55; © Sally Ryan/ZUMA Press/Corbis, p. 56; © John Lamparski/WireImage/Getty Images, p. 59; © Kevin Winter/Getty Images, p. 61; © Chris McGrath/Getty Images, p. 64; © Yoon S. Byun/The Boston Globe/Getty Images, p. 66; Olivier Douliery/MCT/Newscom, p. 68; AP Photo/The Star Tribune/Leila Navidi, p. 73; AP Photo/Carolyn Kaster, p. 76; © Teresa DiGirolamo/Yours Forever Photography; © D Dipasupi/Getty Images for PFLAG, p. 80.

Front cover: © iStockphoto.com/manx_in_the_world (rainbow flag); © iStockphoto.com/efks (grass); © iStockphoto.com/microgen (swimmer).

# ABOUT THE AUTHORS

Kirstin Cronn-Mills, PhD, teaches writing, literature, and critical thinking at South Central College in North Mankato, Minnesota. She writes fiction, poetry, and nonfiction books and articles. Her young adult novels include the Minnesota Book Award finalist *The Sky Always Hears Me and the Hills Don't Mind*, the Lambda Literary Award finalist *Beautiful Music for Ugly Children*, winner of the 2014 American Library Association's Stonewall Book Award, and *Original Fake*, a Junior Library Guild selection. Her nonfiction YA title *Transgender Lives: Complex Stories, Complex Voices* was among the titles selected by the Children's Book Committee at Bank Street College for their 2015 Best YA Books of the Year. It was also featured on the NYC Reads 265 Recommended Reading List in 2015.

Alex Jackson Nelson, MSW, LGSW, NIC, lives in Saint Paul, Minnesota. He has worked with lesbian, gay, bisexual, transgender, queer, and other (LGBTQ+) youth since 1997. Alex is also a nationally certified American Sign Language interpreter.